This Hot Sauce Tasting Log Book

Belongs to

____

DEDICATION

This Hot Sauce Tasting Log Book is dedicated to all the Hot Sauce Lovers out there who are mindful of spicy condiments and want to have fun in the process.

You are my inspiration for producing books and I'm honored to be a part of keeping all of your thoughts and ideas organized all in one easy to find spot.

How to use this Hot Sauce Tasting Log Book:

This ultimate hot sauce tasting notebook is a perfect way to track and record all your spicy condiment tasty activities. This unique hot sauce Journal is a great way to keep all of your important information all in one easy to find spot.

Each interior page includes prompts and space to record the following:

1. Name - Write the name of which hot sauce you are tasting.

2. Origin - Use the box provided to write in who made it, or what company.

3. Scoville - Stay on task using the box to fill in the scale rating from mild to intolerable heat.

4. Color - Record and track the color of the sauce ranging from green, red, yellow to orange.

5. Brand - Use the box to write the brand of hot sauce you are tasting.

6. Sample - Stay on task using the space to write in which sampler, or company the sauce came from.

7. Texture - Record anything from watery to thick dollop to describe the texture.

8. Flavor Wheel - Checklist what flavor was sampled, anywhere from floral to salty.

9. Main Ingredients - Space to write ingredients of the spicy condiment tasted.

10. Heat Meter - Fill in the heat rating of the hot sauce sampled, from mild to heat.

If you are new to hot sauce tasting or have been at it for a while, this hot sauce tasting journal is a must have! Can make a great useful gift for anyone that aspires to be a hot sauce sommelier!

Have Fun!

NAME	BRAND
ORIGIN	SAMPLED
SCOVILLE	TEXTURE
COLOR	PRICE

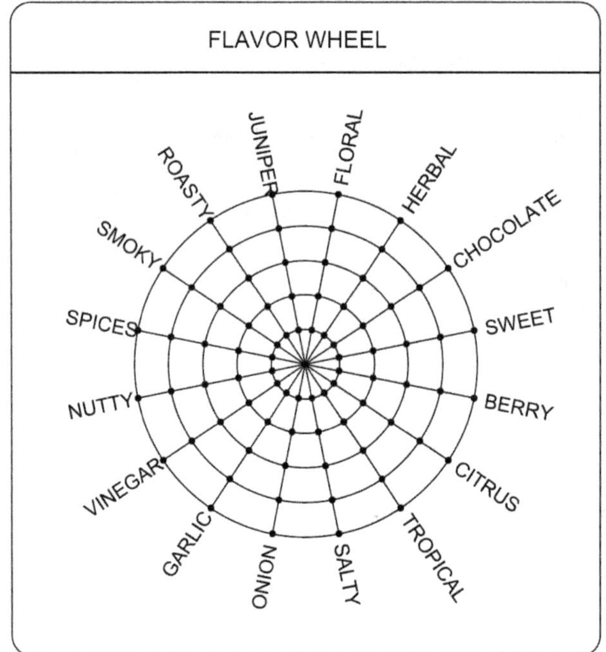

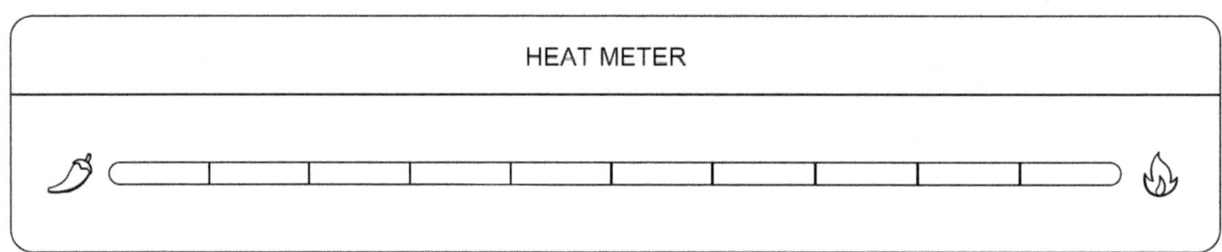

ADDITIONAL NOTES

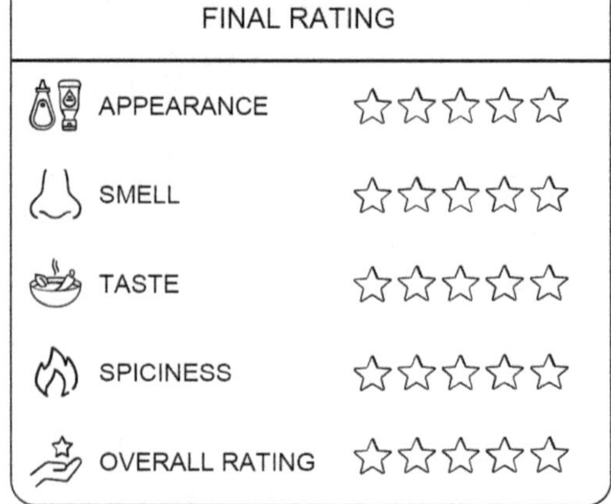

NAME	BRAND
ORIGIN	SAMPLED
SCOVILLE	TEXTURE
COLOR	PRICE

FLAVOR WHEEL

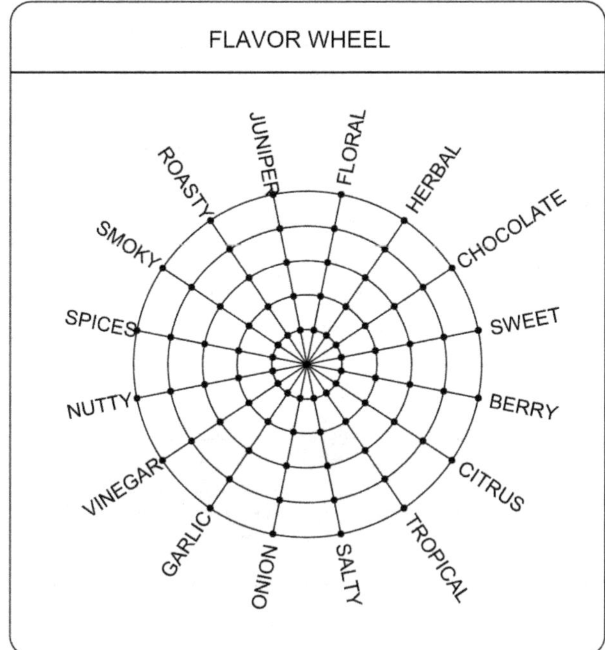

MAIN INGREDIENTS

HEAT METER

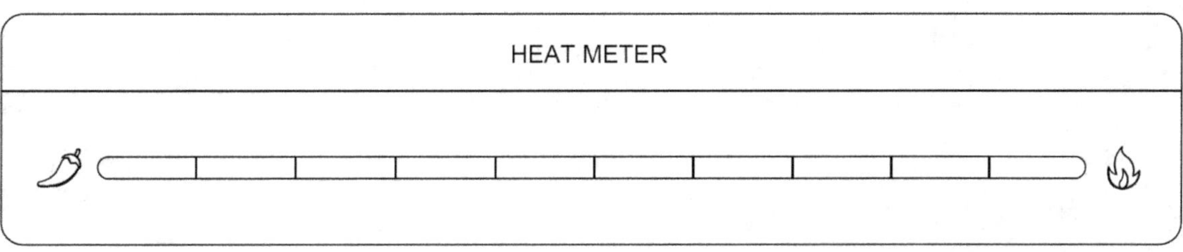

ADDITIONAL NOTES

FINAL RATING

APPEARANCE ☆☆☆☆☆

SMELL ☆☆☆☆☆

TASTE ☆☆☆☆☆

SPICINESS ☆☆☆☆☆

OVERALL RATING ☆☆☆☆☆

NAME	BRAND
ORIGIN	SAMPLED
SCOVILLE	TEXTURE
COLOR	PRICE

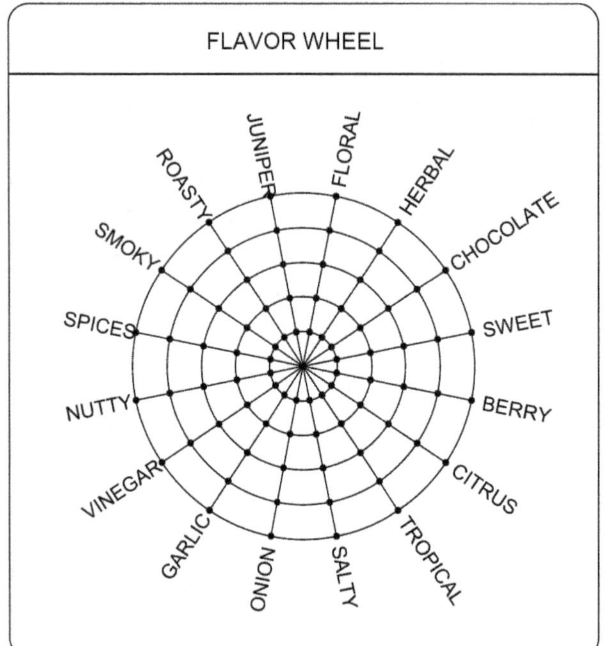

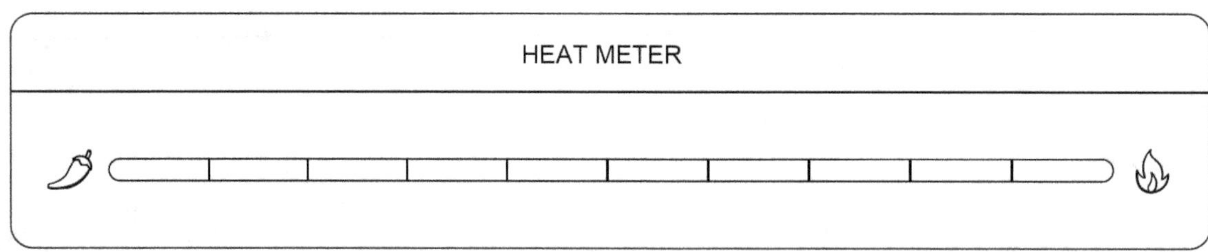

ADDITIONAL NOTES

NAME	BRAND
ORIGIN	SAMPLED
SCOVILLE	TEXTURE
COLOR	PRICE

FLAVOR WHEEL

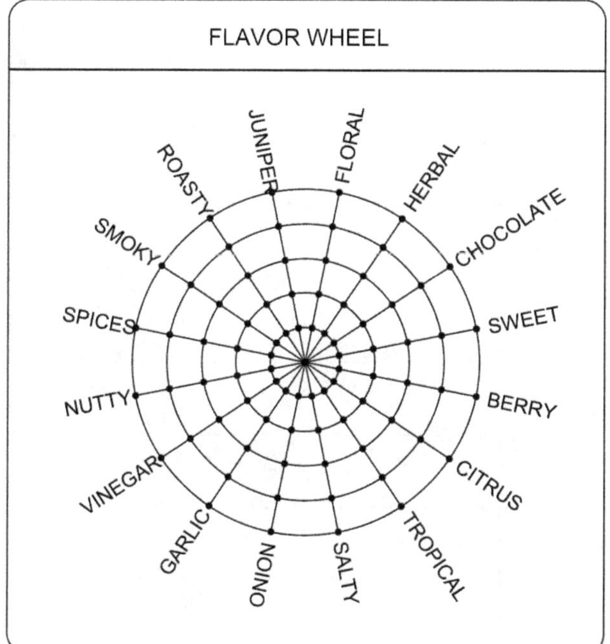

MAIN INGREDIENTS

HEAT METER

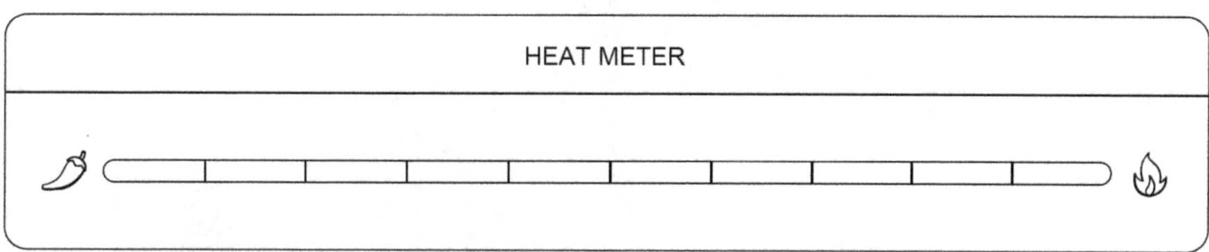

ADDITIONAL NOTES

FINAL RATING	
APPEARANCE	☆☆☆☆☆
SMELL	☆☆☆☆☆
TASTE	☆☆☆☆☆
SPICINESS	☆☆☆☆☆
OVERALL RATING	☆☆☆☆☆

NAME	BRAND
ORIGIN	SAMPLED
SCOVILLE	TEXTURE
COLOR	PRICE

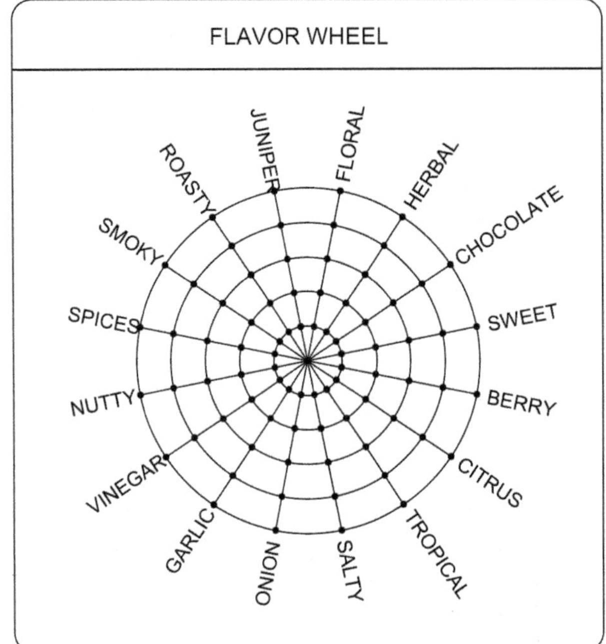

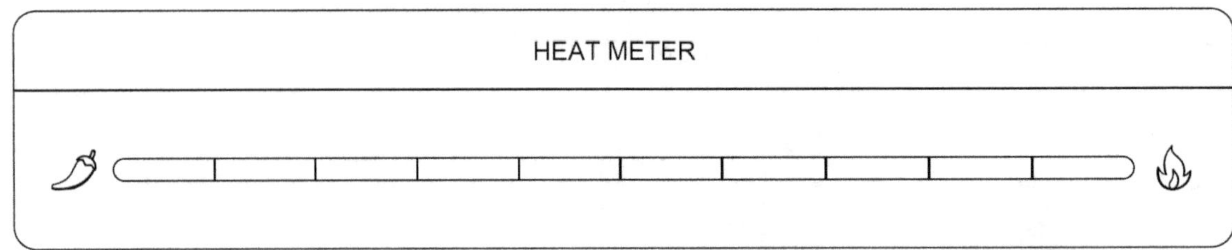

ADDITIONAL NOTES

FINAL RATING

APPEARANCE ☆☆☆☆☆

SMELL ☆☆☆☆☆

TASTE ☆☆☆☆☆

SPICINESS ☆☆☆☆☆

OVERALL RATING ☆☆☆☆☆

NAME	BRAND
ORIGIN	SAMPLED
SCOVILLE	TEXTURE
COLOR	PRICE

FLAVOR WHEEL

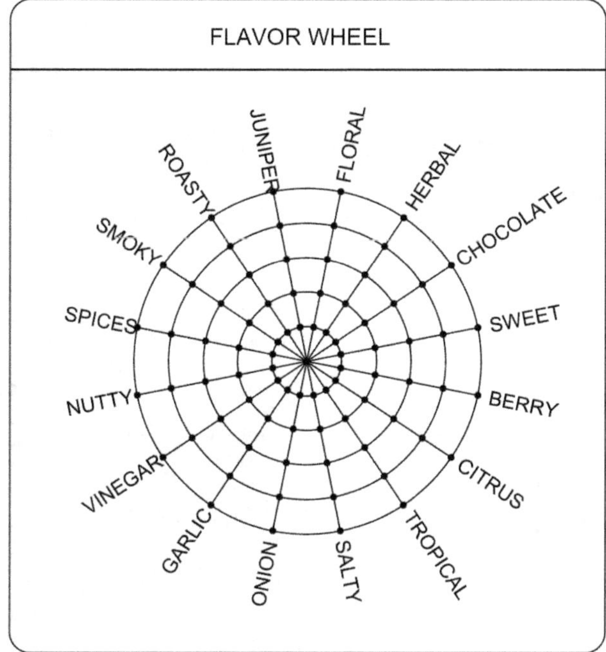

MAIN INGREDIENTS

HEAT METER

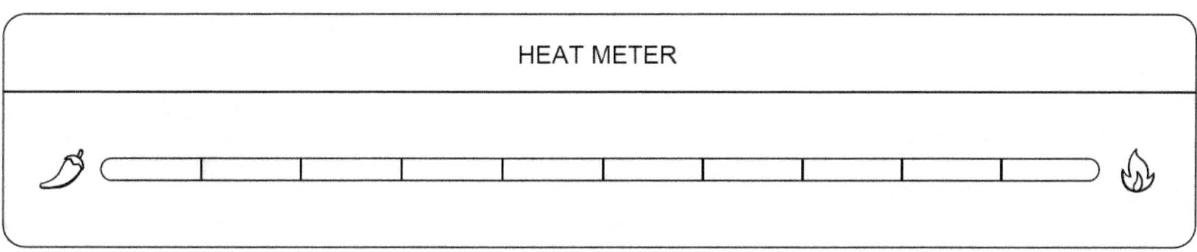

ADDITIONAL NOTES

FINAL RATING

APPEARANCE ☆☆☆☆☆

SMELL ☆☆☆☆☆

TASTE ☆☆☆☆☆

SPICINESS ☆☆☆☆☆

OVERALL RATING ☆☆☆☆☆

NAME	BRAND
ORIGIN	SAMPLED
SCOVILLE	TEXTURE
COLOR	PRICE

FLAVOR WHEEL

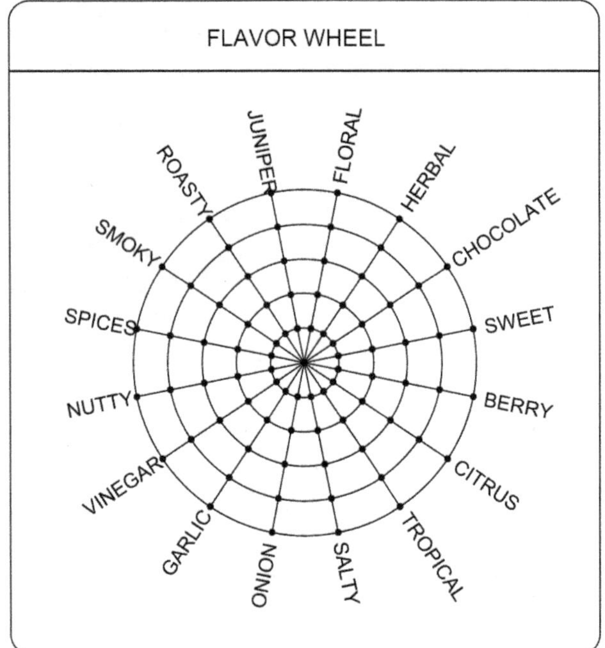

MAIN INGREDIENTS

HEAT METER

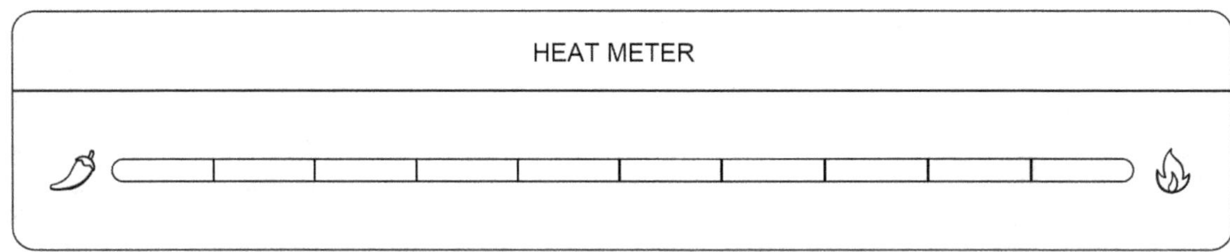

ADDITIONAL NOTES

FINAL RATING

NAME	BRAND
ORIGIN	SAMPLED
SCOVILLE	TEXTURE
COLOR	PRICE

FLAVOR WHEEL

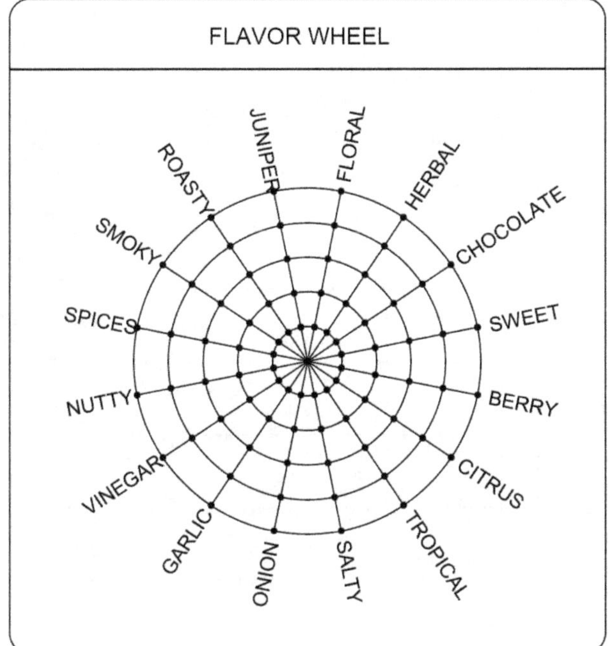

MAIN INGREDIENTS

HEAT METER

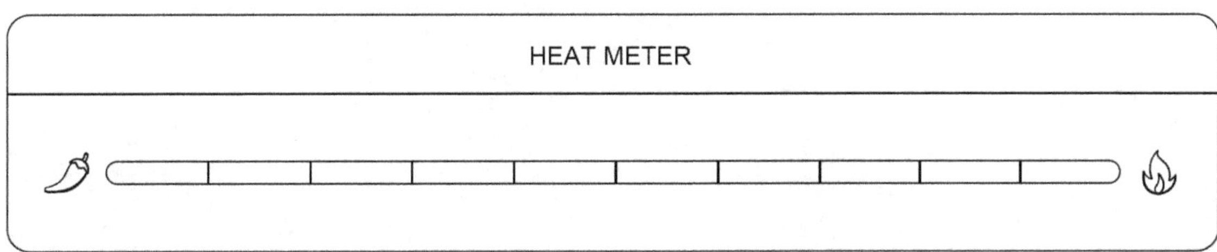

ADDITIONAL NOTES

FINAL RATING

APPEARANCE ☆☆☆☆☆

SMELL ☆☆☆☆☆

TASTE ☆☆☆☆☆

SPICINESS ☆☆☆☆☆

OVERALL RATING ☆☆☆☆☆

NAME	BRAND
ORIGIN	SAMPLED
SCOVILLE	TEXTURE
COLOR	PRICE

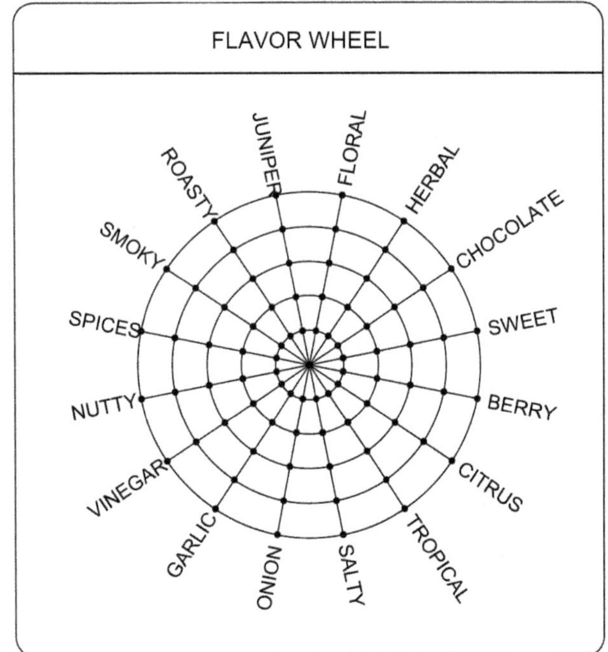

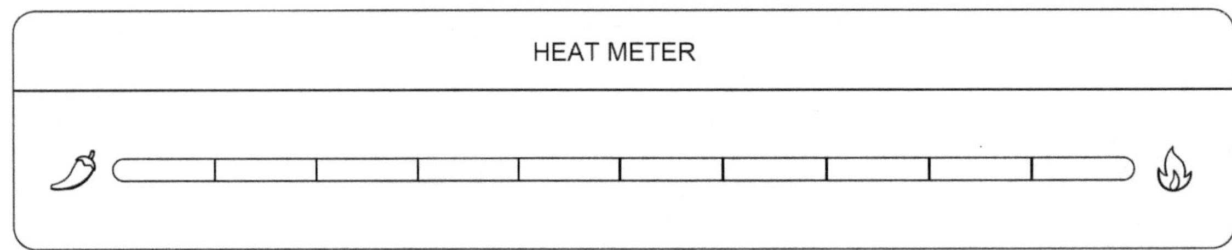

ADDITIONAL NOTES

FINAL RATING

APPEARANCE ☆☆☆☆☆

SMELL ☆☆☆☆☆

TASTE ☆☆☆☆☆

SPICINESS ☆☆☆☆☆

OVERALL RATING ☆☆☆☆☆

NAME	BRAND
ORIGIN	SAMPLED
SCOVILLE	TEXTURE
COLOR	PRICE

FLAVOR WHEEL

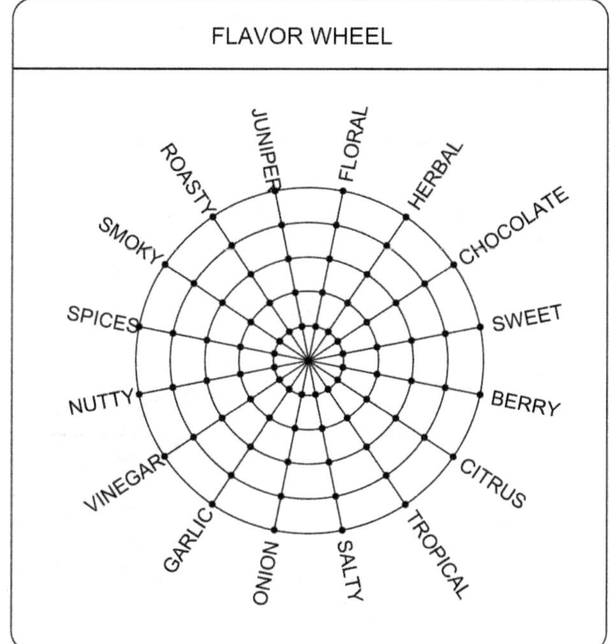

MAIN INGREDIENTS

HEAT METER

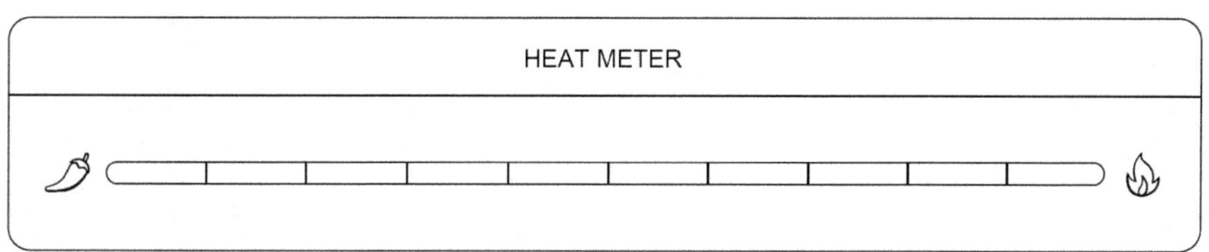

ADDITIONAL NOTES

FINAL RATING

APPEARANCE ☆☆☆☆☆

SMELL ☆☆☆☆☆

TASTE ☆☆☆☆☆

SPICINESS ☆☆☆☆☆

OVERALL RATING ☆☆☆☆☆

NAME	BRAND
ORIGIN	SAMPLED
SCOVILLE	TEXTURE
COLOR	PRICE

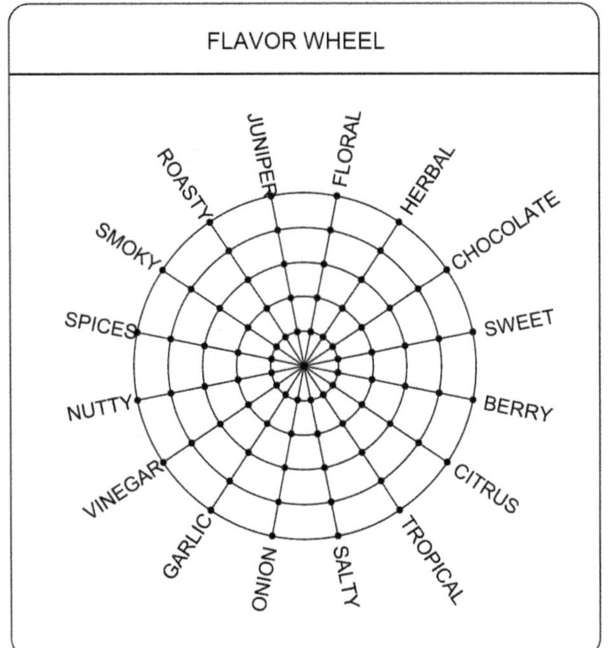

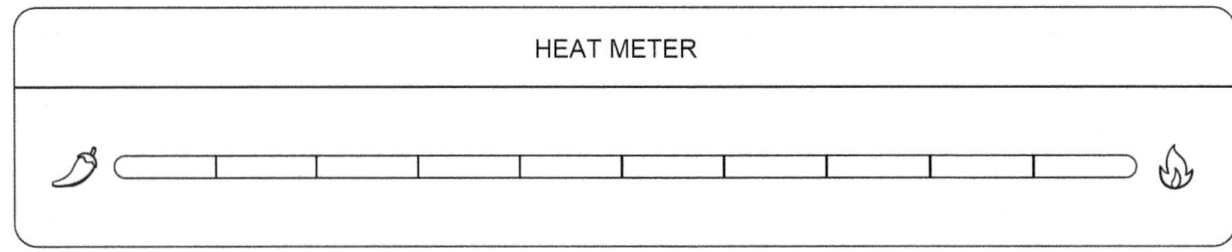

ADDITIONAL NOTES

NAME	BRAND
ORIGIN	SAMPLED
SCOVILLE	TEXTURE
COLOR	PRICE

FLAVOR WHEEL

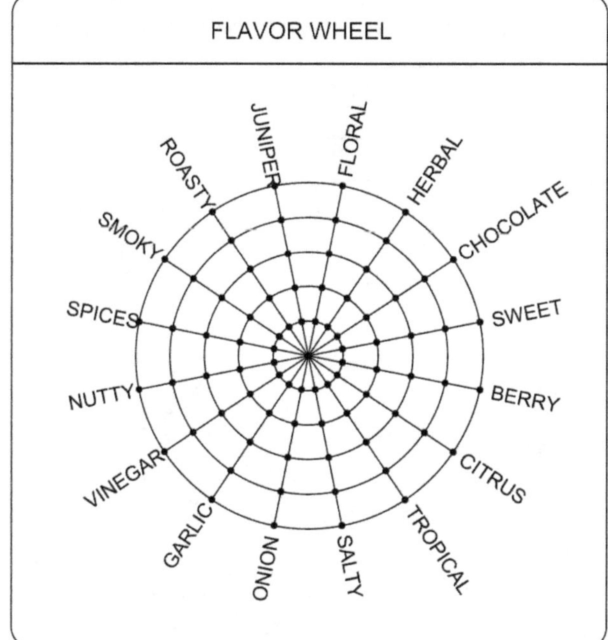

MAIN INGREDIENTS

HEAT METER

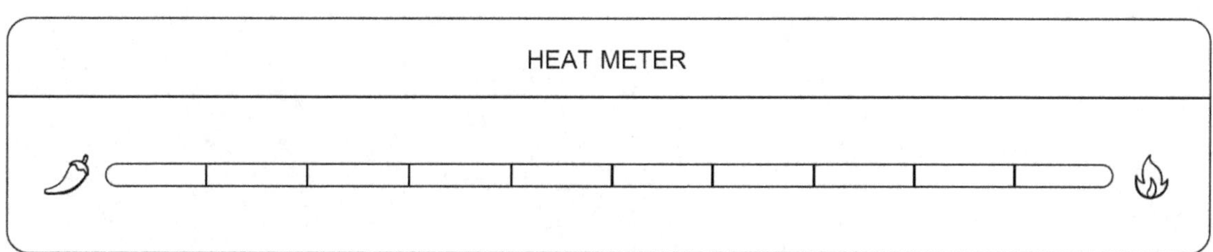

ADDITIONAL NOTES

FINAL RATING

APPEARANCE ☆☆☆☆☆

SMELL ☆☆☆☆☆

TASTE ☆☆☆☆☆

SPICINESS ☆☆☆☆☆

OVERALL RATING ☆☆☆☆☆

NAME	BRAND
ORIGIN	SAMPLED
SCOVILLE	TEXTURE
COLOR	PRICE

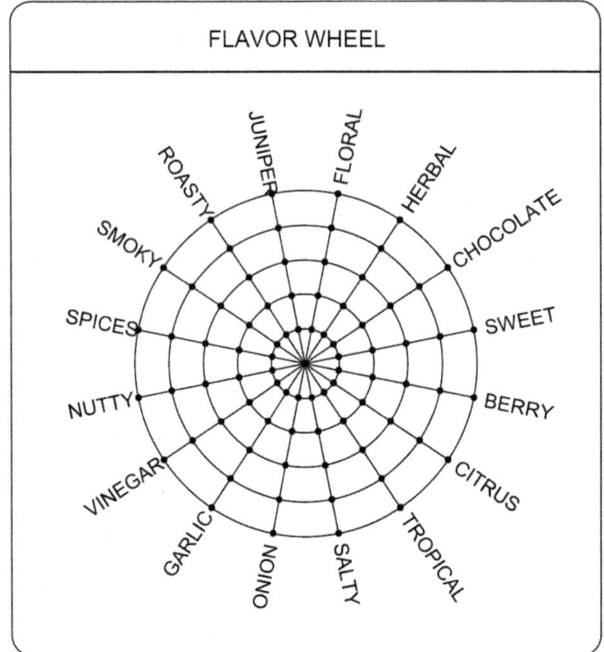

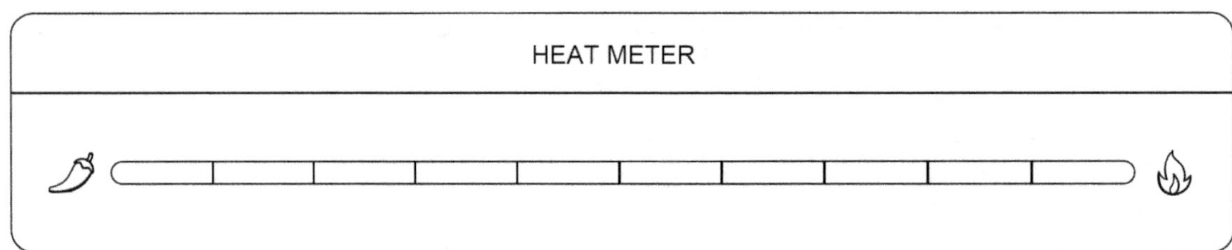

ADDITIONAL NOTES

NAME	BRAND
ORIGIN	SAMPLED
SCOVILLE	TEXTURE
COLOR	PRICE

FLAVOR WHEEL

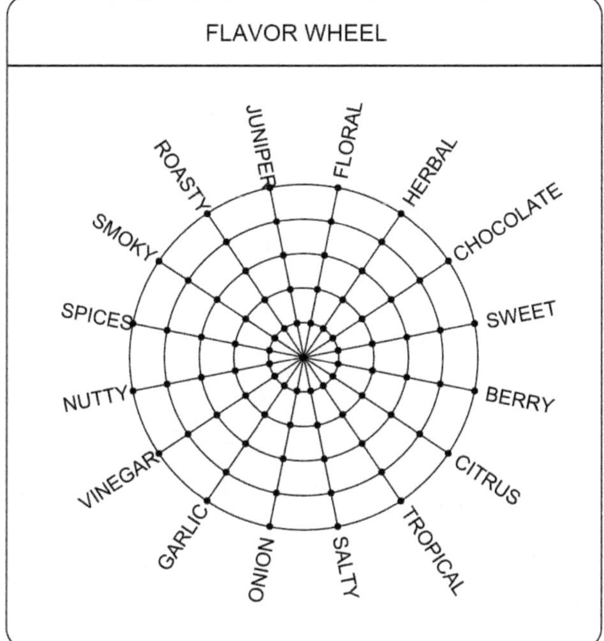

MAIN INGREDIENTS

HEAT METER

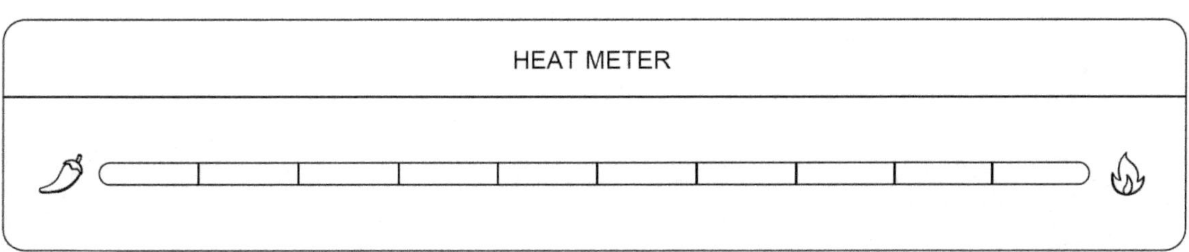

ADDITIONAL NOTES

FINAL RATING

APPEARANCE ☆☆☆☆☆

SMELL ☆☆☆☆☆

TASTE ☆☆☆☆☆

SPICINESS ☆☆☆☆☆

OVERALL RATING ☆☆☆☆☆

NAME	BRAND
ORIGIN	SAMPLED
SCOVILLE	TEXTURE
COLOR	PRICE

FLAVOR WHEEL

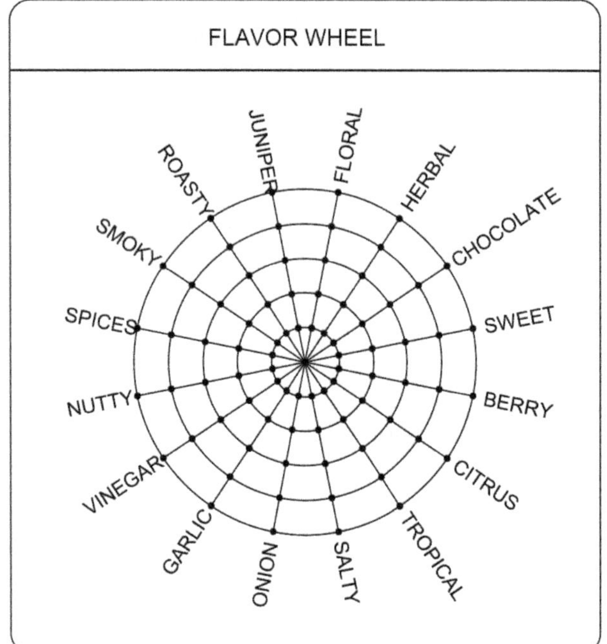

MAIN INGREDIENTS

HEAT METER

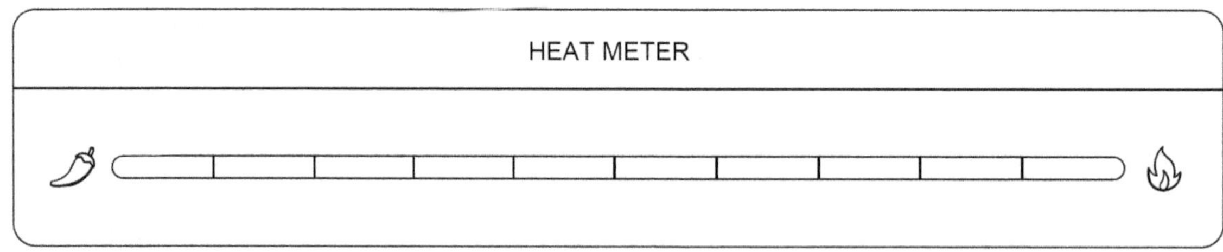

ADDITIONAL NOTES

FINAL RATING

NAME	BRAND
ORIGIN	SAMPLED
SCOVILLE	TEXTURE
COLOR	PRICE

FLAVOR WHEEL

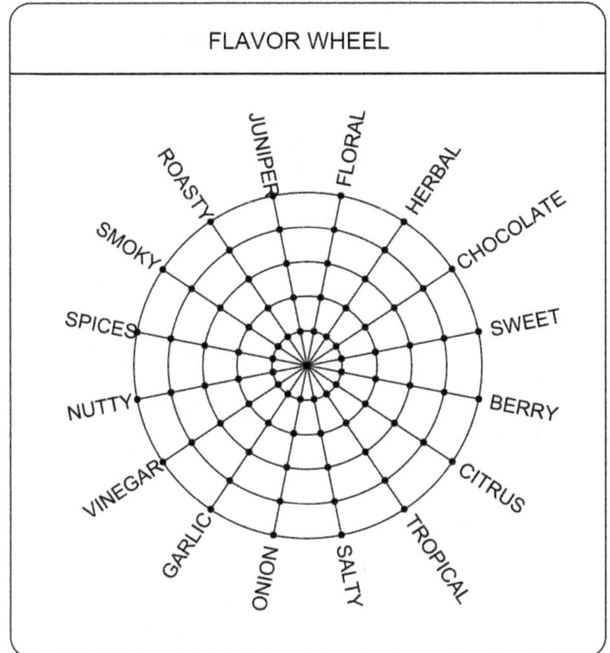

MAIN INGREDIENTS

HEAT METER

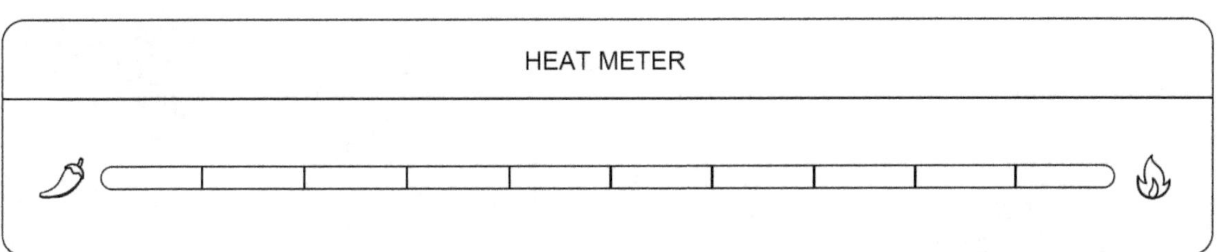

ADDITIONAL NOTES

FINAL RATING

APPEARANCE ☆☆☆☆☆

SMELL ☆☆☆☆☆

TASTE ☆☆☆☆☆

SPICINESS ☆☆☆☆☆

OVERALL RATING ☆☆☆☆☆

NAME	BRAND
ORIGIN	SAMPLED
SCOVILLE	TEXTURE
COLOR	PRICE

FLAVOR WHEEL

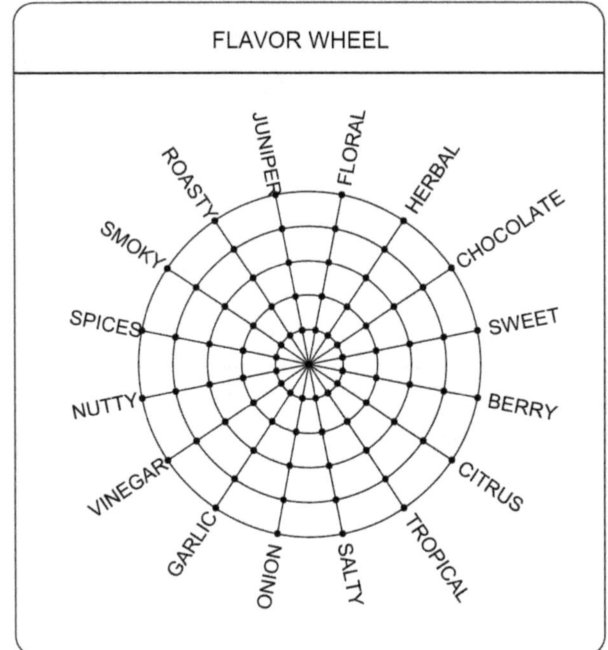

MAIN INGREDIENTS

HEAT METER

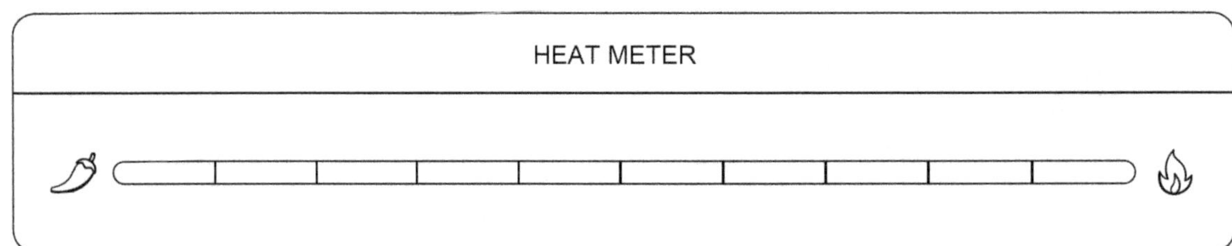

ADDITIONAL NOTES

FINAL RATING

NAME	BRAND
ORIGIN	SAMPLED
SCOVILLE	TEXTURE
COLOR	PRICE

FLAVOR WHEEL

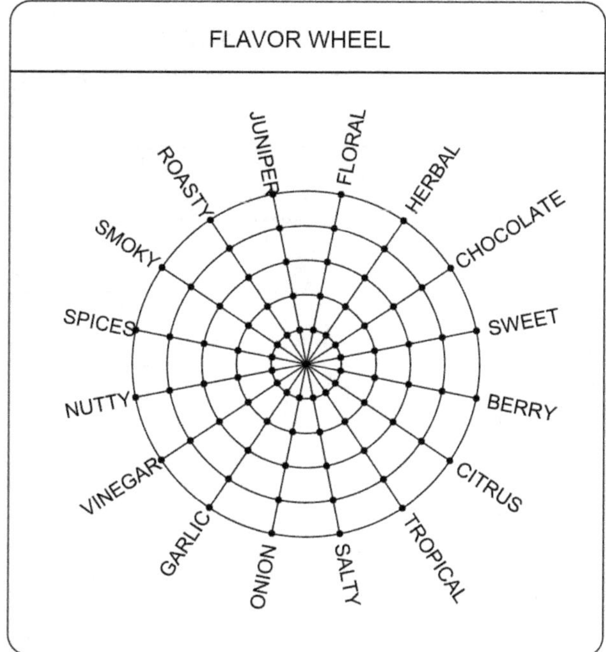

MAIN INGREDIENTS

HEAT METER

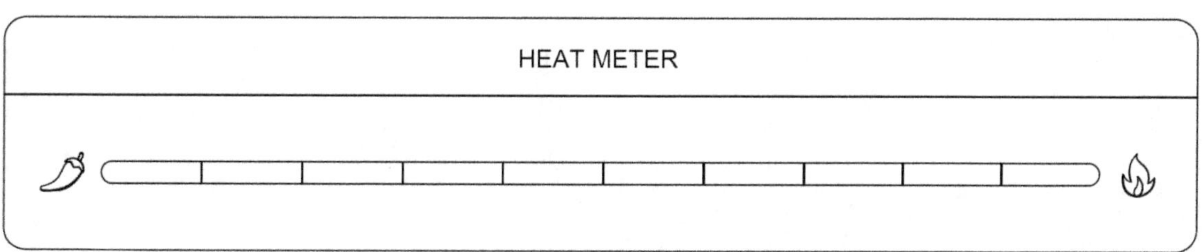

ADDITIONAL NOTES

FINAL RATING

APPEARANCE	☆☆☆☆☆
SMELL	☆☆☆☆☆
TASTE	☆☆☆☆☆
SPICINESS	☆☆☆☆☆
OVERALL RATING	☆☆☆☆☆

NAME	BRAND
ORIGIN	SAMPLED
SCOVILLE	TEXTURE
COLOR	PRICE

FLAVOR WHEEL

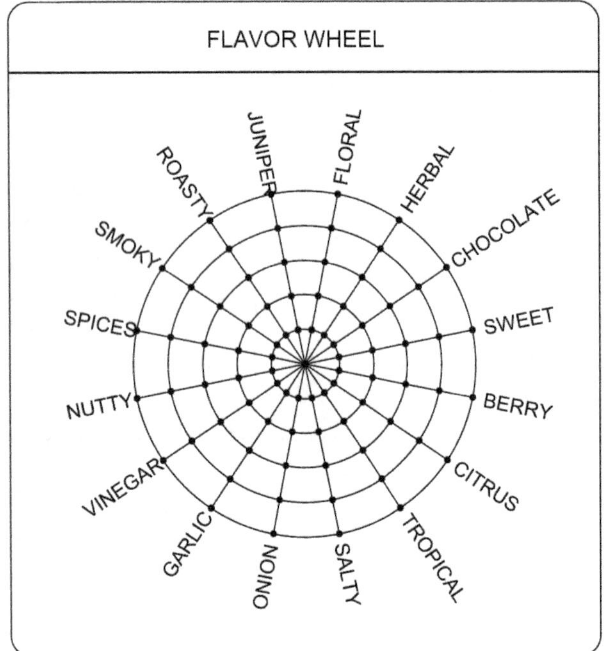

MAIN INGREDIENTS

HEAT METER

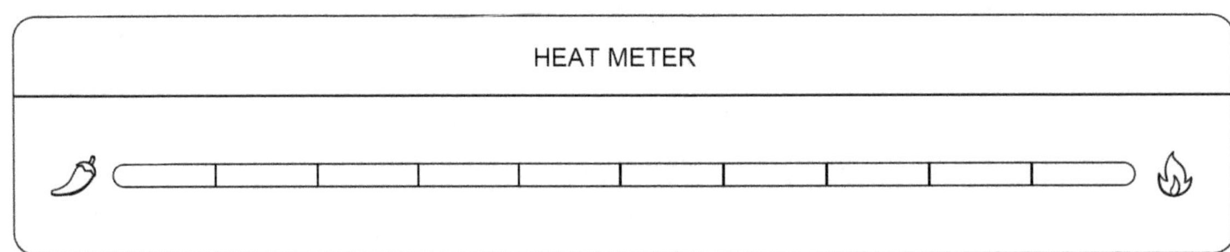

ADDITIONAL NOTES

FINAL RATING

NAME	BRAND
ORIGIN	SAMPLED
SCOVILLE	TEXTURE
COLOR	PRICE

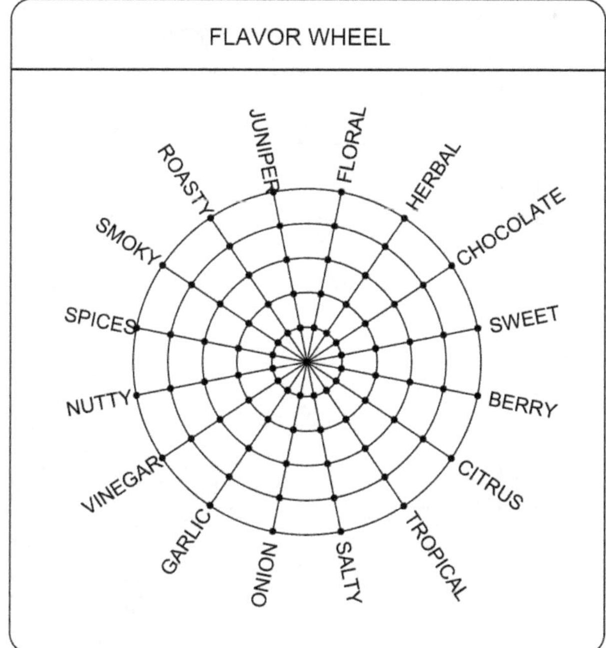

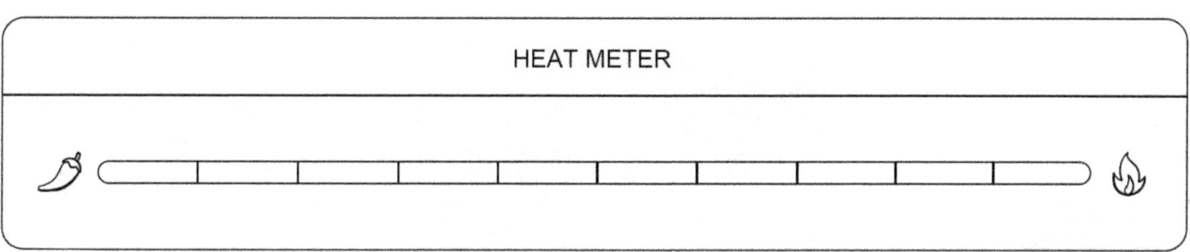

ADDITIONAL NOTES

FINAL RATING

APPEARANCE ☆☆☆☆☆

SMELL ☆☆☆☆☆

TASTE ☆☆☆☆☆

SPICINESS ☆☆☆☆☆

OVERALL RATING ☆☆☆☆☆

NAME	BRAND
ORIGIN	SAMPLED
SCOVILLE	TEXTURE
COLOR	PRICE

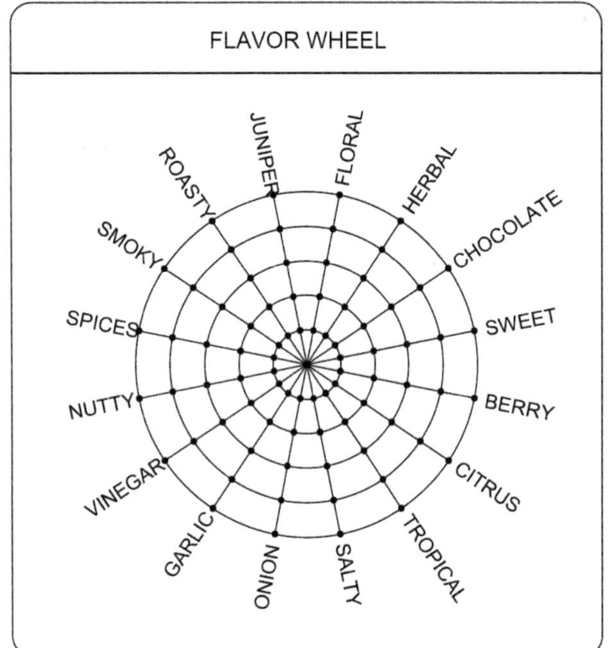

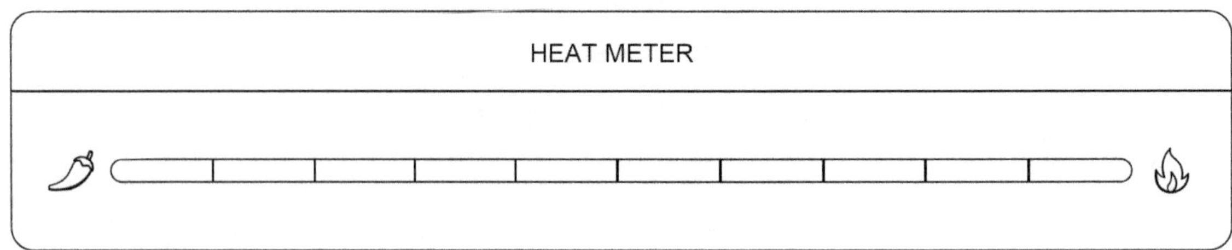

ADDITIONAL NOTES

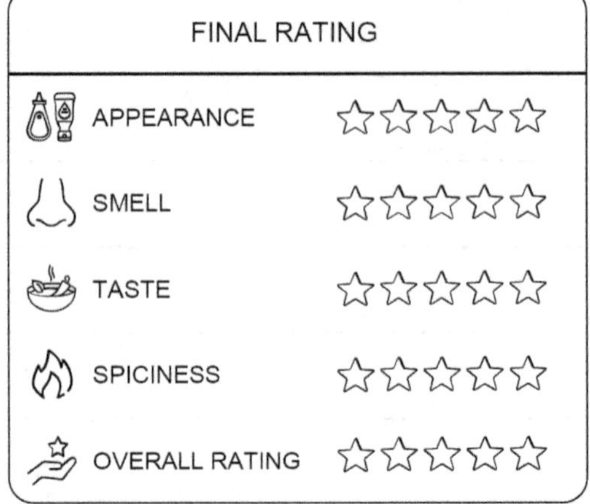

NAME	BRAND
ORIGIN	SAMPLED
SCOVILLE	TEXTURE
COLOR	PRICE

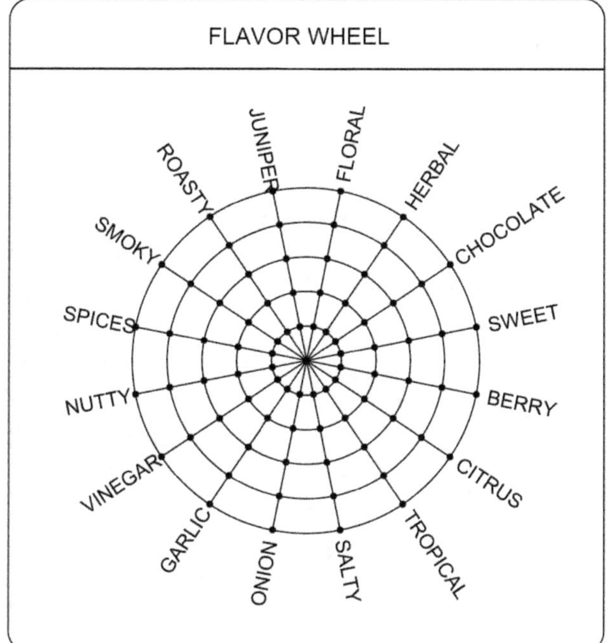

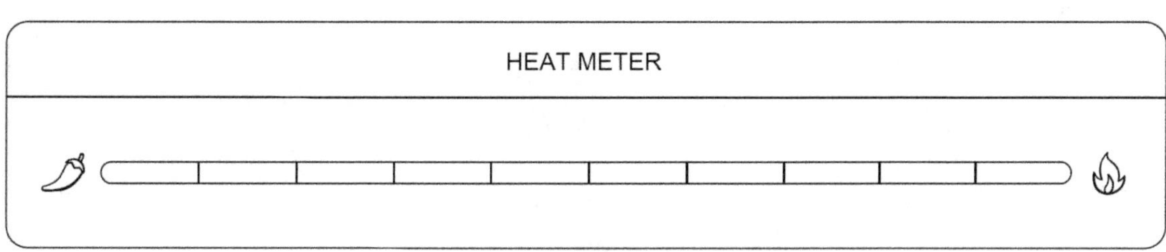

ADDITIONAL NOTES

FINAL RATING

APPEARANCE ☆☆☆☆☆

SMELL ☆☆☆☆☆

TASTE ☆☆☆☆☆

SPICINESS ☆☆☆☆☆

OVERALL RATING ☆☆☆☆☆

NAME	BRAND
ORIGIN	SAMPLED
SCOVILLE	TEXTURE
COLOR	PRICE

FLAVOR WHEEL

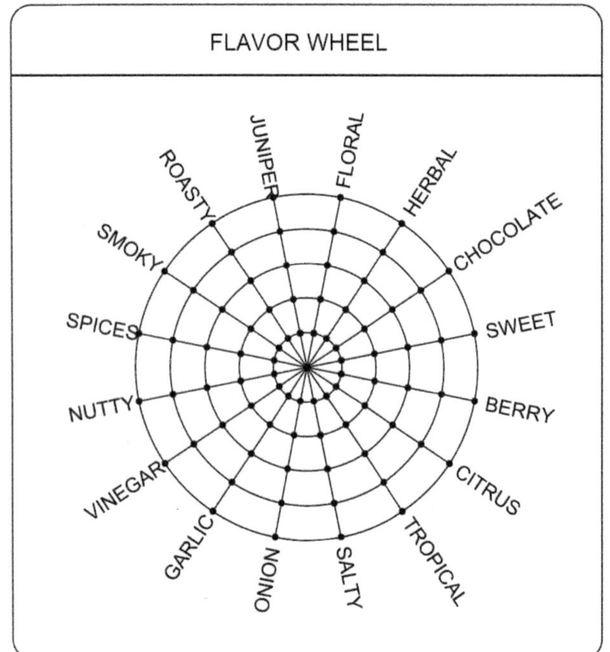

MAIN INGREDIENTS

HEAT METER

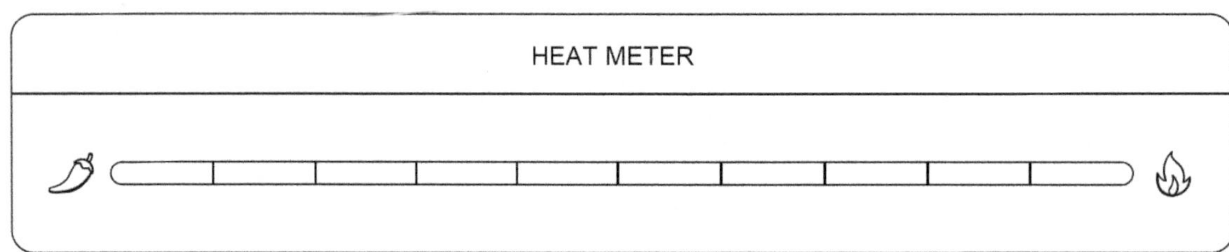

ADDITIONAL NOTES

FINAL RATING

NAME	BRAND
ORIGIN	SAMPLED
SCOVILLE	TEXTURE
COLOR	PRICE

FLAVOR WHEEL

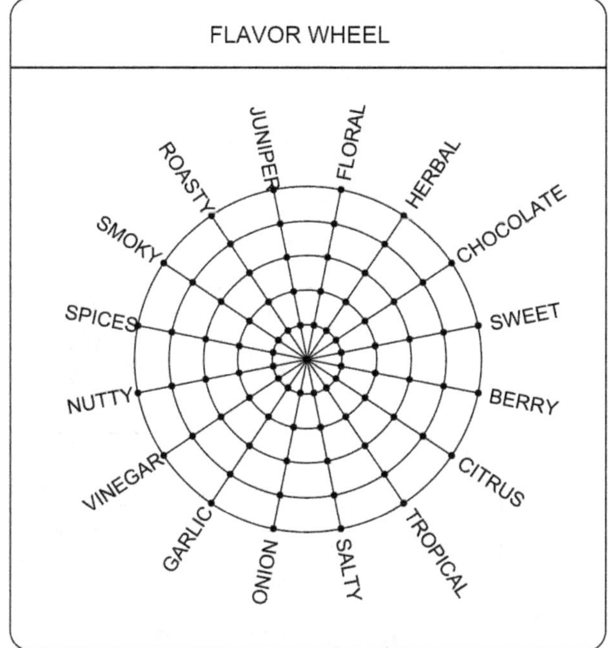

MAIN INGREDIENTS

HEAT METER

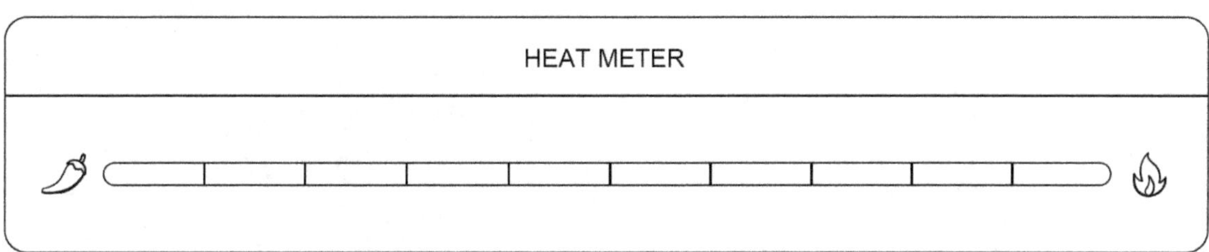

ADDITIONAL NOTES

FINAL RATING

APPEARANCE	☆☆☆☆☆
SMELL	☆☆☆☆☆
TASTE	☆☆☆☆☆
SPICINESS	☆☆☆☆☆
OVERALL RATING	☆☆☆☆☆

NAME	BRAND
ORIGIN	SAMPLED
SCOVILLE	TEXTURE
COLOR	PRICE

FLAVOR WHEEL

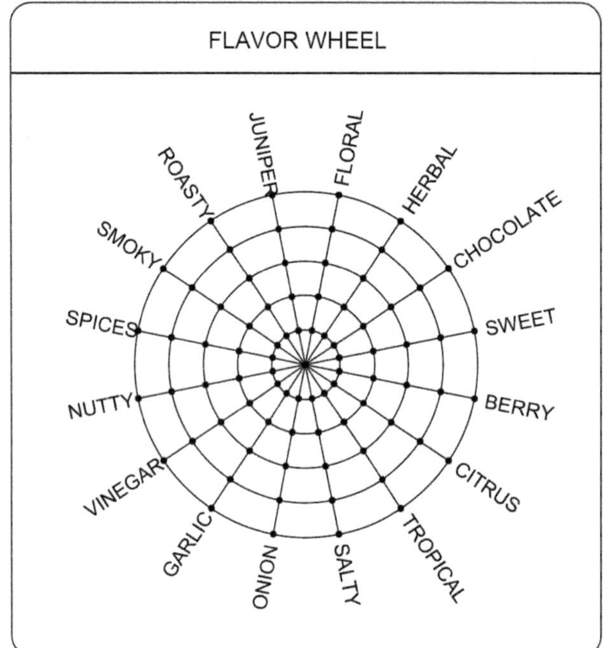

MAIN INGREDIENTS

HEAT METER

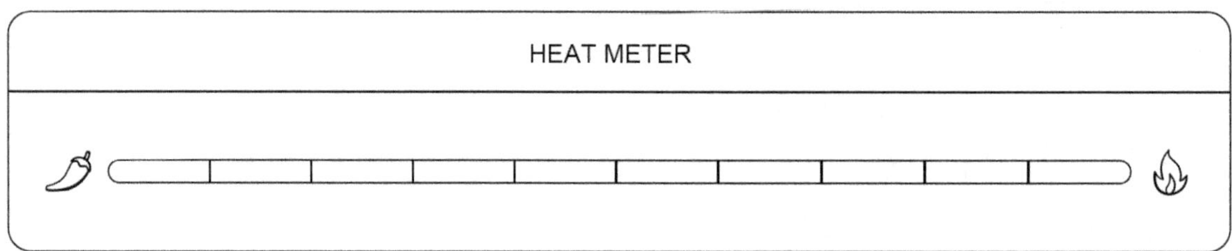

ADDITIONAL NOTES

FINAL RATING

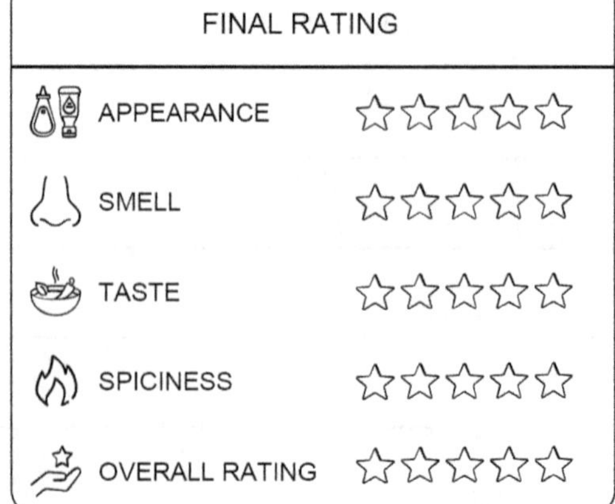

NAME	BRAND
ORIGIN	SAMPLED
SCOVILLE	TEXTURE
COLOR	PRICE

FLAVOR WHEEL

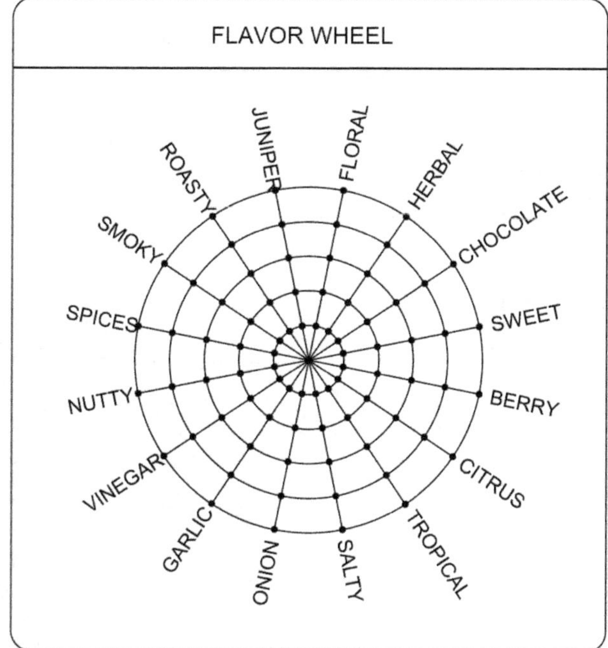

MAIN INGREDIENTS

HEAT METER

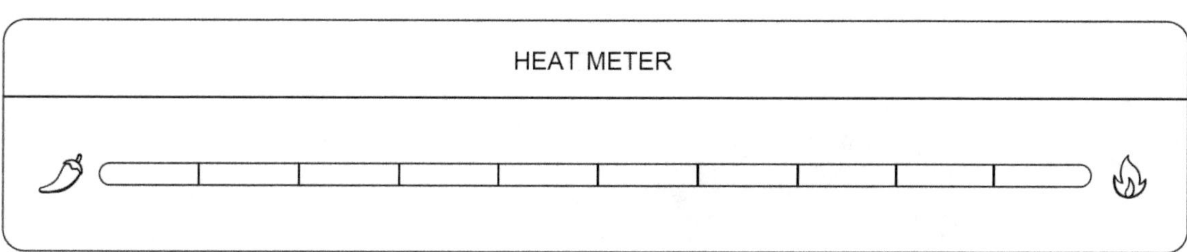

ADDITIONAL NOTES

FINAL RATING

APPEARANCE ☆☆☆☆☆

SMELL ☆☆☆☆☆

TASTE ☆☆☆☆☆

SPICINESS ☆☆☆☆☆

OVERALL RATING ☆☆☆☆☆

NAME	BRAND
ORIGIN	SAMPLED
SCOVILLE	TEXTURE
COLOR	PRICE

FLAVOR WHEEL

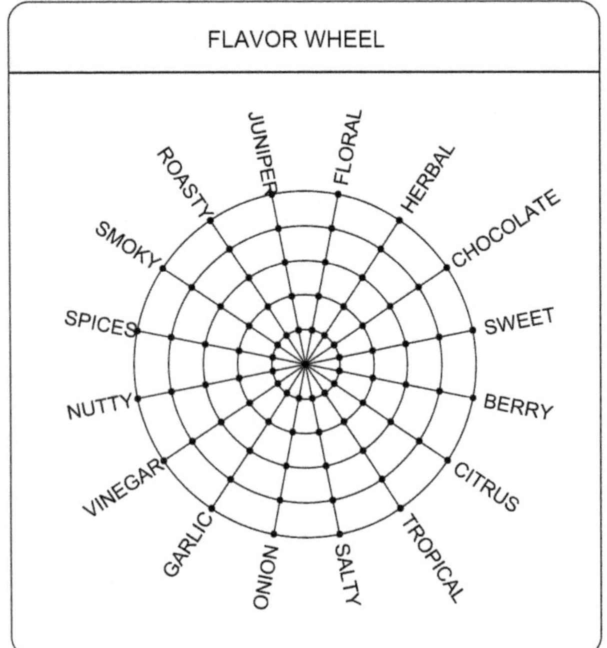

MAIN INGREDIENTS

HEAT METER

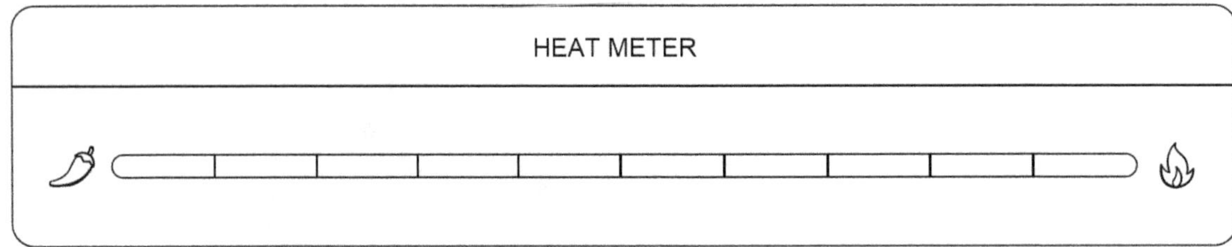

ADDITIONAL NOTES

FINAL RATING

APPEARANCE ☆☆☆☆☆

SMELL ☆☆☆☆☆

TASTE ☆☆☆☆☆

SPICINESS ☆☆☆☆☆

OVERALL RATING ☆☆☆☆☆

NAME	BRAND
ORIGIN	SAMPLED
SCOVILLE	TEXTURE
COLOR	PRICE

FLAVOR WHEEL

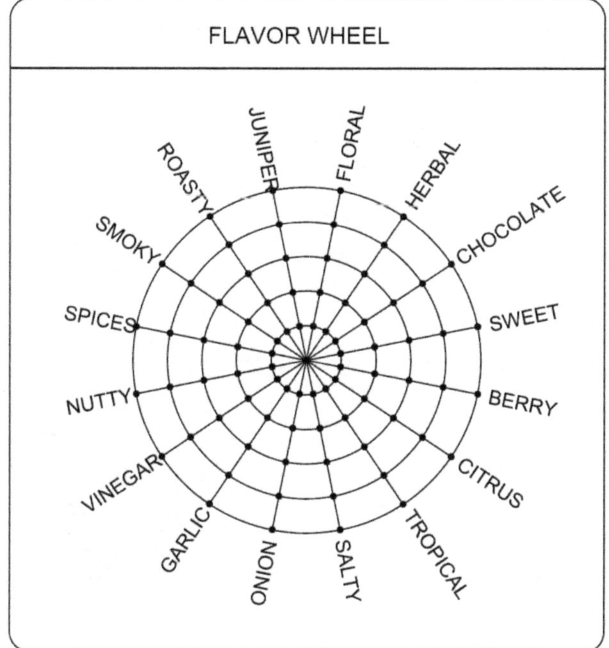

MAIN INGREDIENTS

HEAT METER

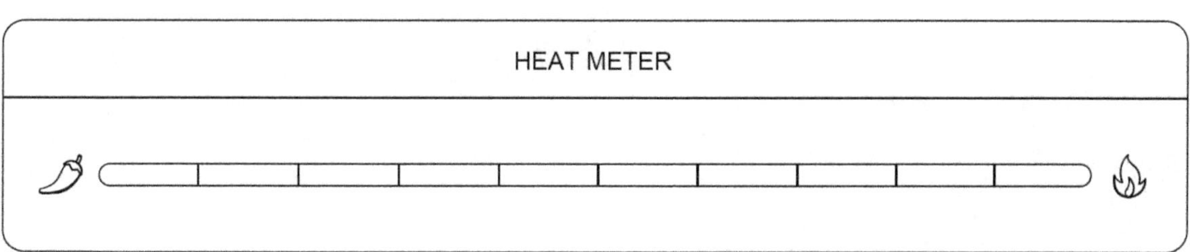

ADDITIONAL NOTES

FINAL RATING

APPEARANCE ☆☆☆☆☆

SMELL ☆☆☆☆☆

TASTE ☆☆☆☆☆

SPICINESS ☆☆☆☆☆

OVERALL RATING ☆☆☆☆☆

NAME	BRAND
ORIGIN	SAMPLED
SCOVILLE	TEXTURE
COLOR	PRICE

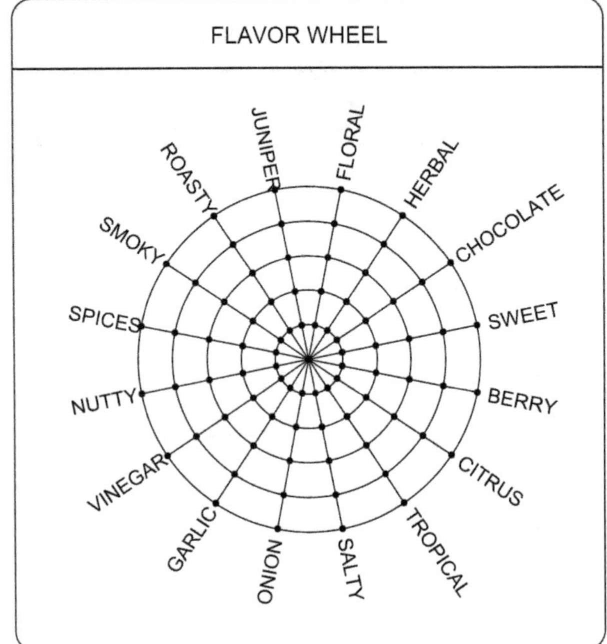

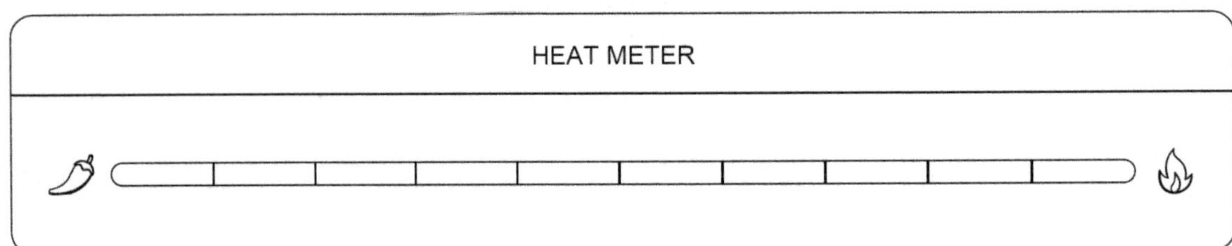

ADDITIONAL NOTES

NAME	BRAND
ORIGIN	SAMPLED
SCOVILLE	TEXTURE
COLOR	PRICE

FLAVOR WHEEL

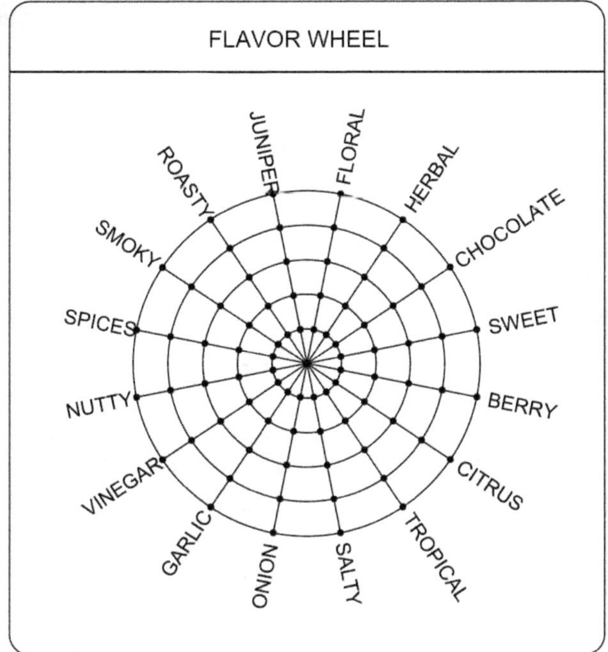

MAIN INGREDIENTS

HEAT METER

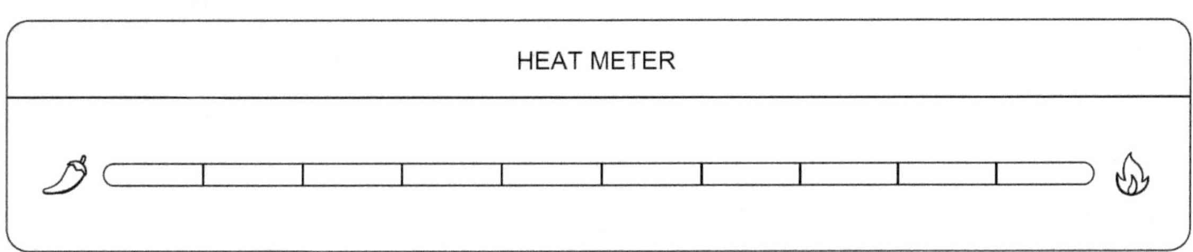

ADDITIONAL NOTES

FINAL RATING

APPEARANCE ☆☆☆☆☆

SMELL ☆☆☆☆☆

TASTE ☆☆☆☆☆

SPICINESS ☆☆☆☆☆

OVERALL RATING ☆☆☆☆☆

NAME	BRAND
ORIGIN	SAMPLED
SCOVILLE	TEXTURE
COLOR	PRICE

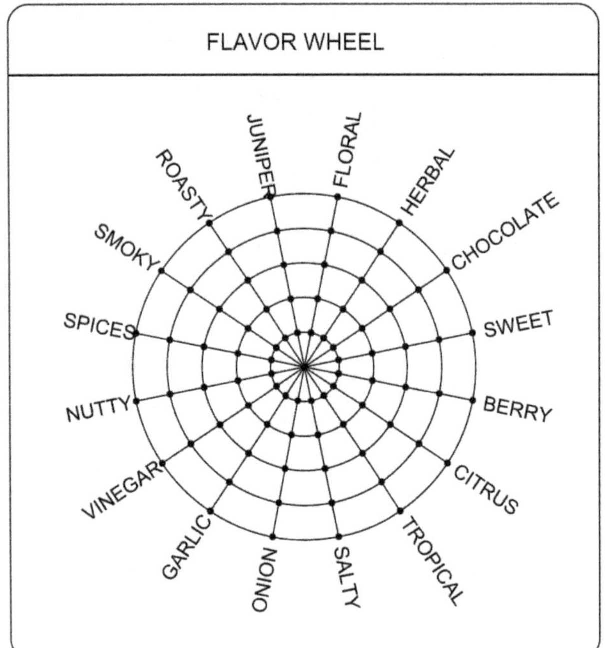

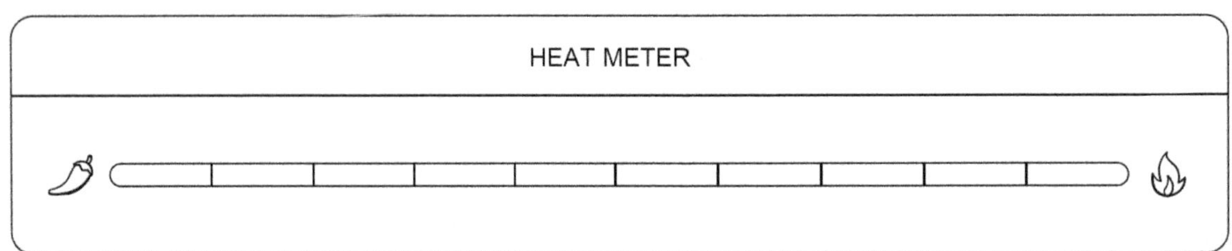

ADDITIONAL NOTES

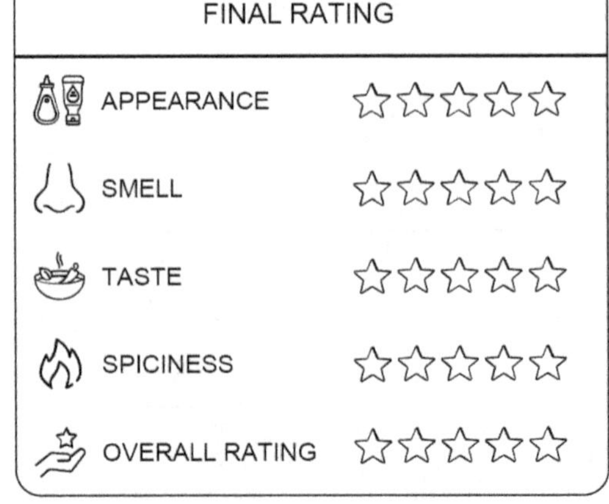

NAME	BRAND
ORIGIN	SAMPLED
SCOVILLE	TEXTURE
COLOR	PRICE

FLAVOR WHEEL

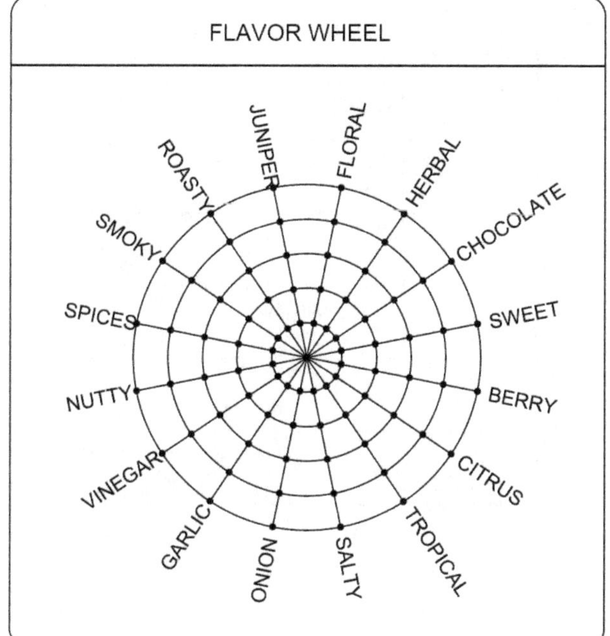

MAIN INGREDIENTS

HEAT METER

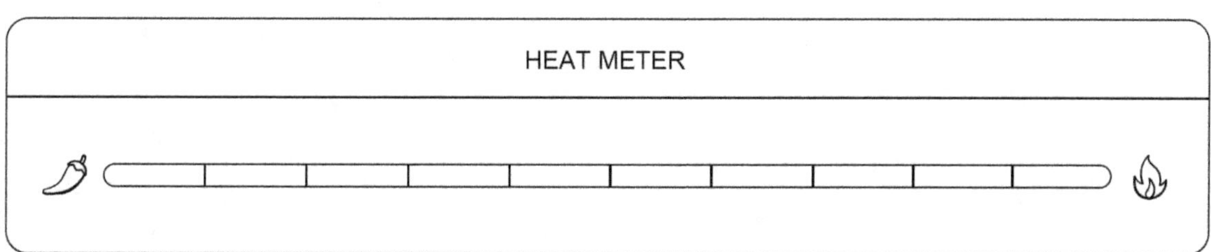

ADDITIONAL NOTES

FINAL RATING

APPEARANCE ☆☆☆☆☆

SMELL ☆☆☆☆☆

TASTE ☆☆☆☆☆

SPICINESS ☆☆☆☆☆

OVERALL RATING ☆☆☆☆☆

NAME	BRAND
ORIGIN	SAMPLED
SCOVILLE	TEXTURE
COLOR	PRICE

FLAVOR WHEEL

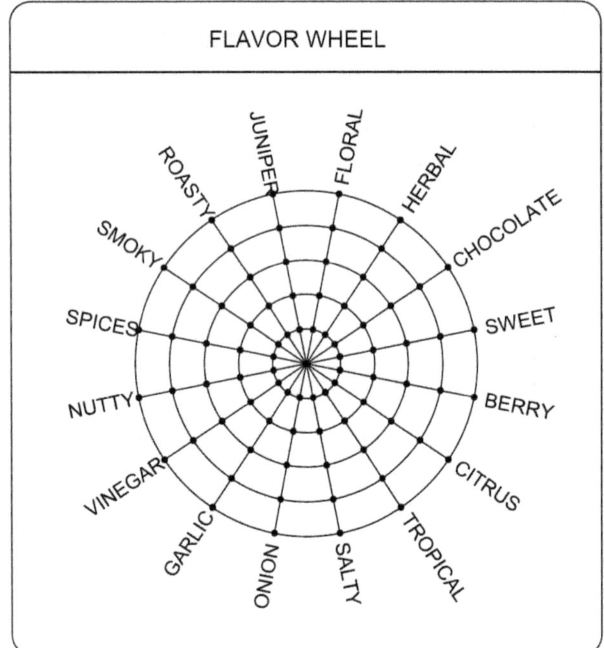

MAIN INGREDIENTS

HEAT METER

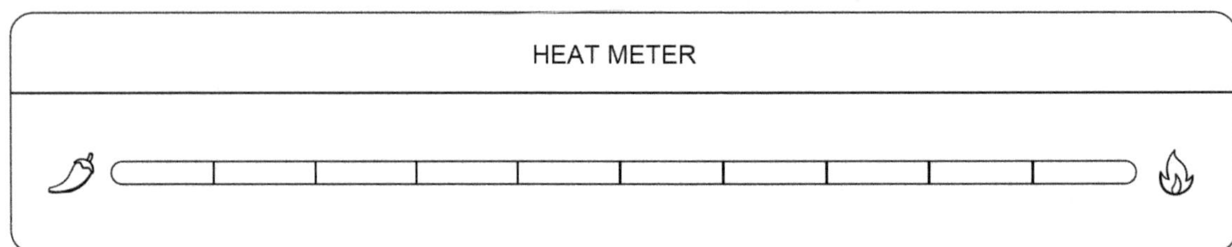

ADDITIONAL NOTES

FINAL RATING

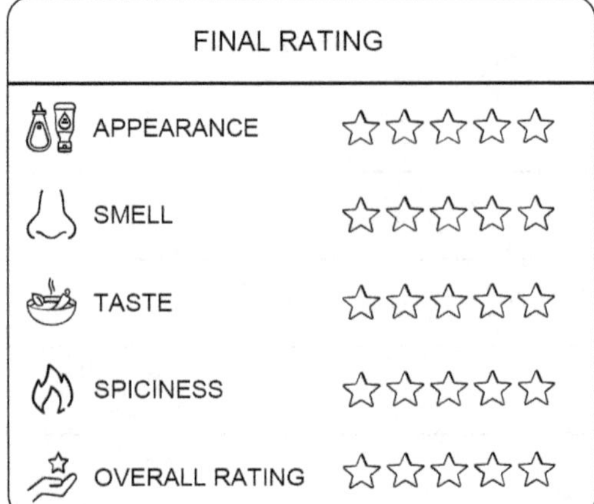

NAME	BRAND
ORIGIN	SAMPLED
SCOVILLE	TEXTURE
COLOR	PRICE

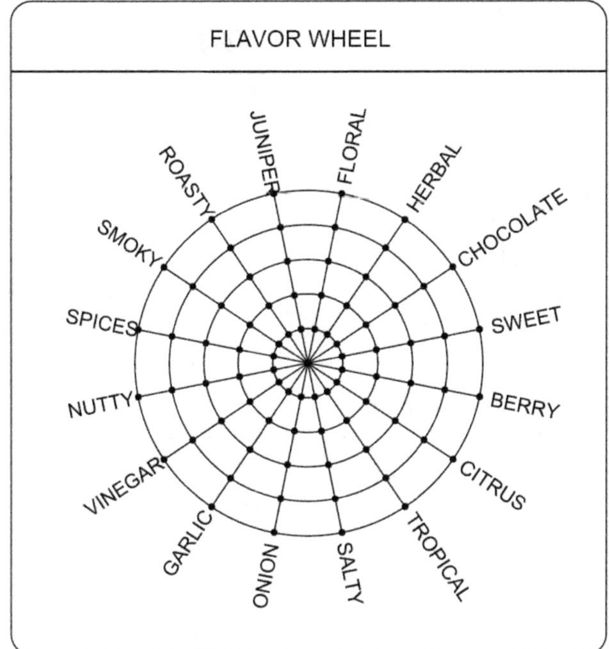

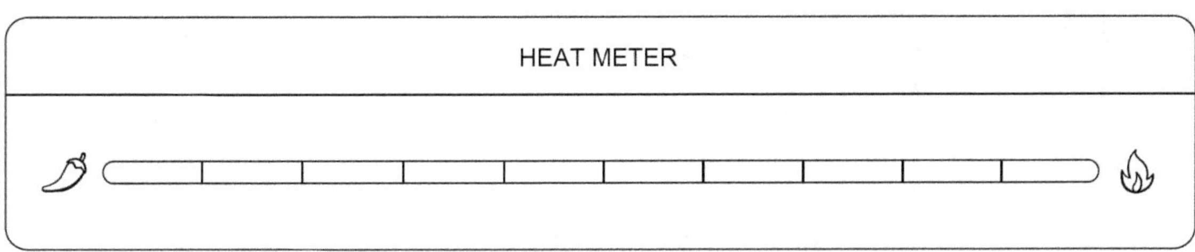

ADDITIONAL NOTES

FINAL RATING

APPEARANCE ☆☆☆☆☆

SMELL ☆☆☆☆☆

TASTE ☆☆☆☆☆

SPICINESS ☆☆☆☆☆

OVERALL RATING ☆☆☆☆☆

NAME	BRAND
ORIGIN	SAMPLED
SCOVILLE	TEXTURE
COLOR	PRICE

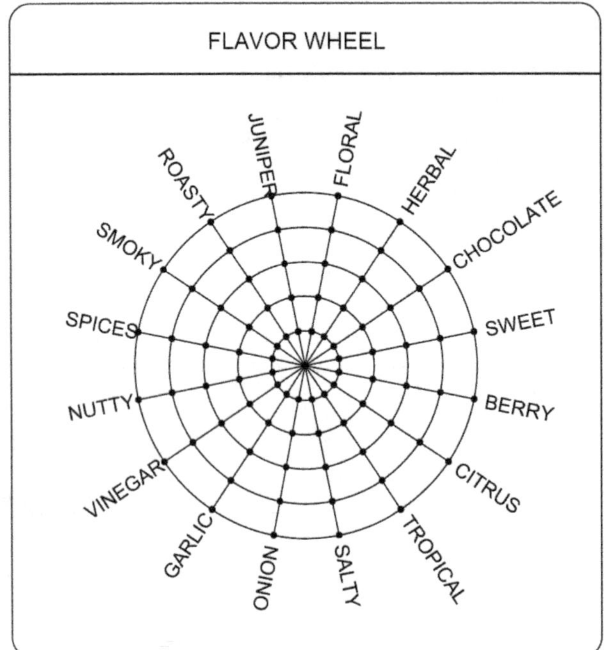

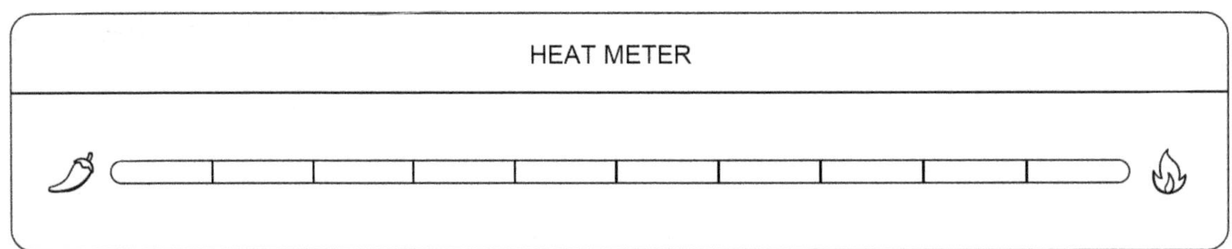

ADDITIONAL NOTES

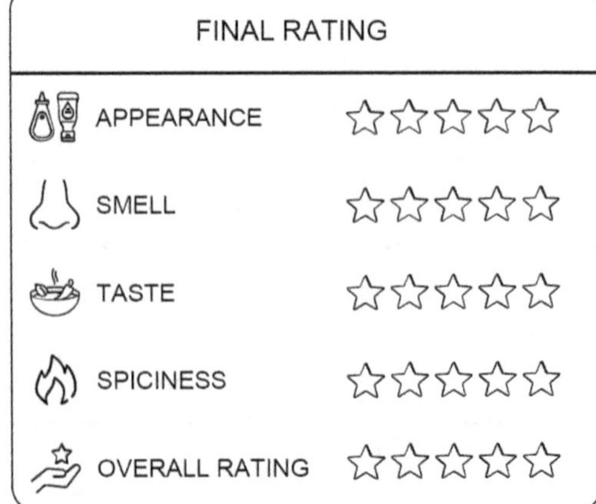

NAME	BRAND
ORIGIN	SAMPLED
SCOVILLE	TEXTURE
COLOR	PRICE

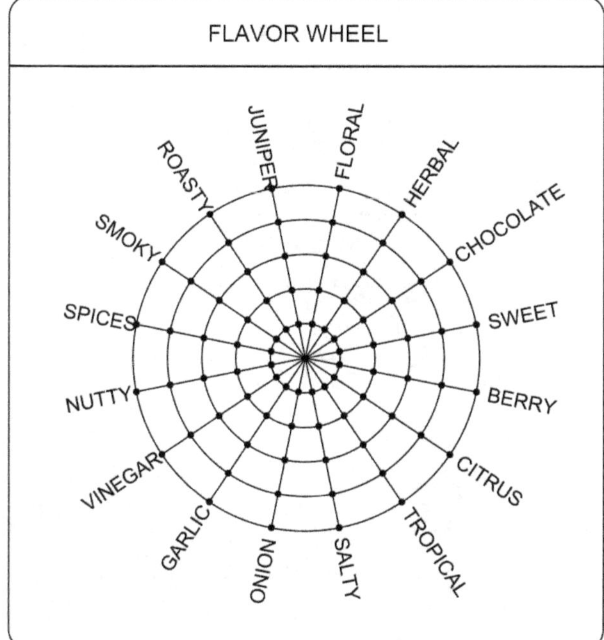

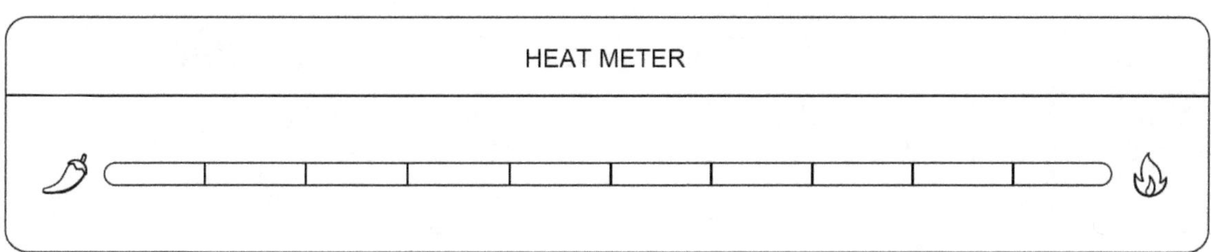

ADDITIONAL NOTES

FINAL RATING

APPEARANCE	☆☆☆☆☆
SMELL	☆☆☆☆☆
TASTE	☆☆☆☆☆
SPICINESS	☆☆☆☆☆
OVERALL RATING	☆☆☆☆☆

NAME	BRAND
ORIGIN	SAMPLED
SCOVILLE	TEXTURE
COLOR	PRICE

FLAVOR WHEEL

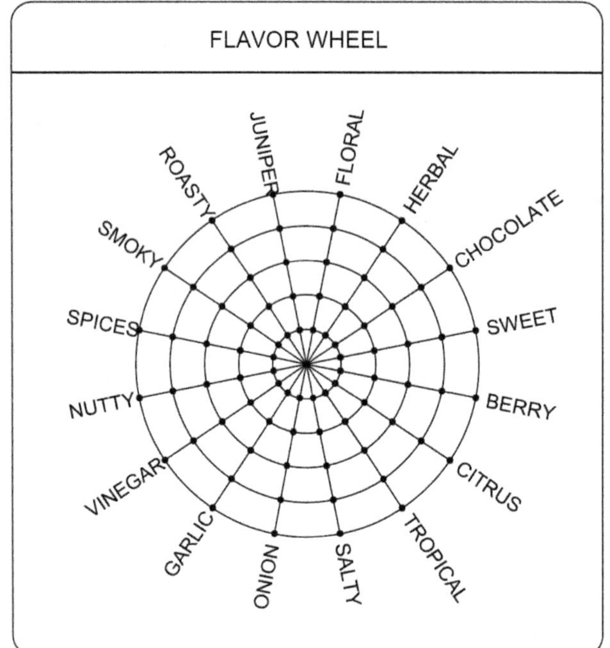

MAIN INGREDIENTS

HEAT METER

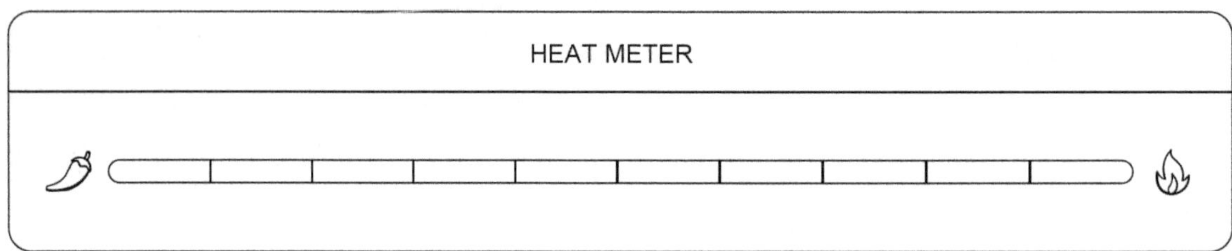

ADDITIONAL NOTES

FINAL RATING

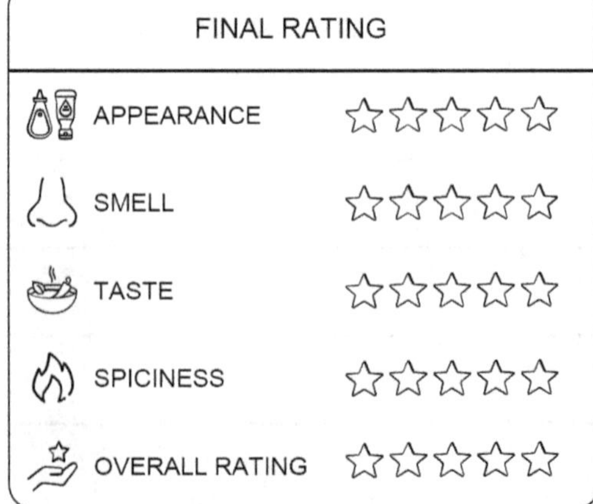

NAME	BRAND
ORIGIN	SAMPLED
SCOVILLE	TEXTURE
COLOR	PRICE

FLAVOR WHEEL

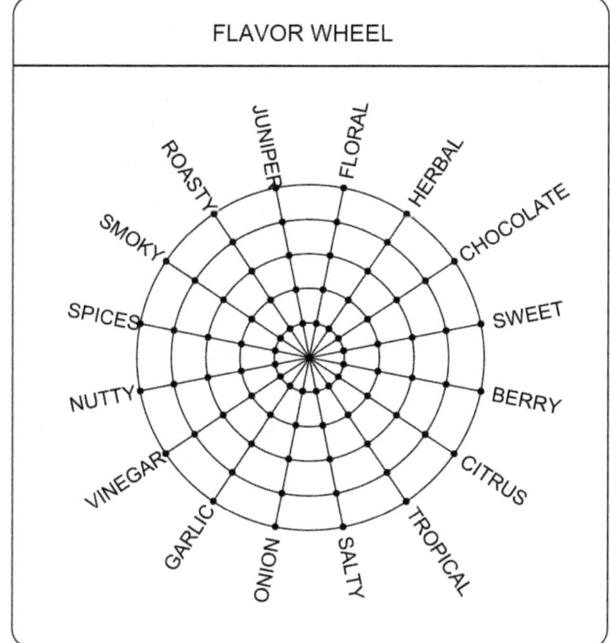

MAIN INGREDIENTS

HEAT METER

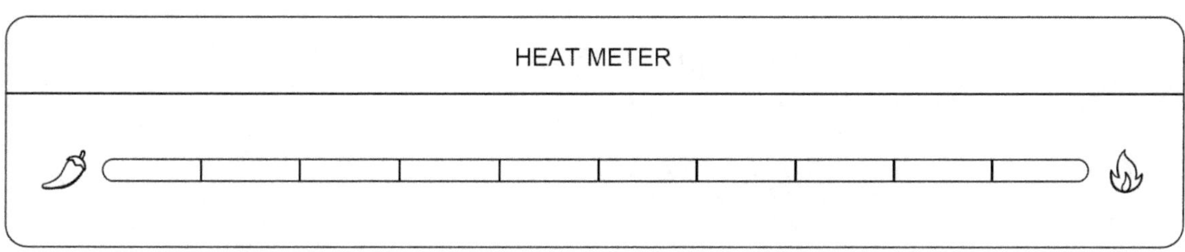

ADDITIONAL NOTES

FINAL RATING

APPEARANCE ☆☆☆☆☆

SMELL ☆☆☆☆☆

TASTE ☆☆☆☆☆

SPICINESS ☆☆☆☆☆

OVERALL RATING ☆☆☆☆☆

NAME	BRAND
ORIGIN	SAMPLED
SCOVILLE	TEXTURE
COLOR	PRICE

FLAVOR WHEEL

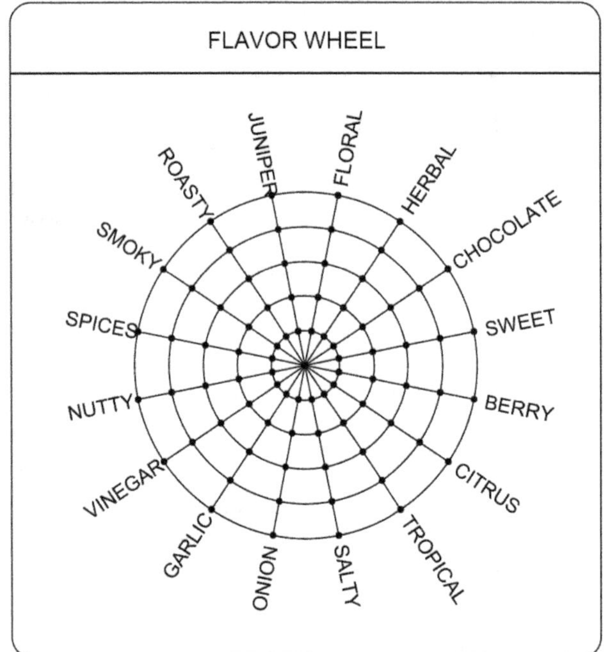

MAIN INGREDIENTS

HEAT METER

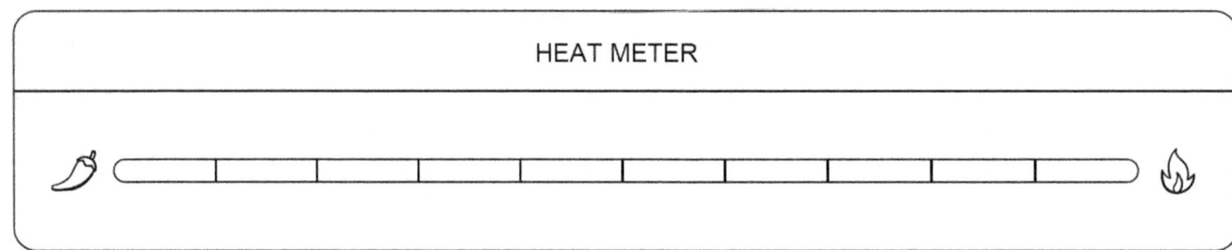

ADDITIONAL NOTES

FINAL RATING

NAME	BRAND
ORIGIN	SAMPLED
SCOVILLE	TEXTURE
COLOR	PRICE

FLAVOR WHEEL

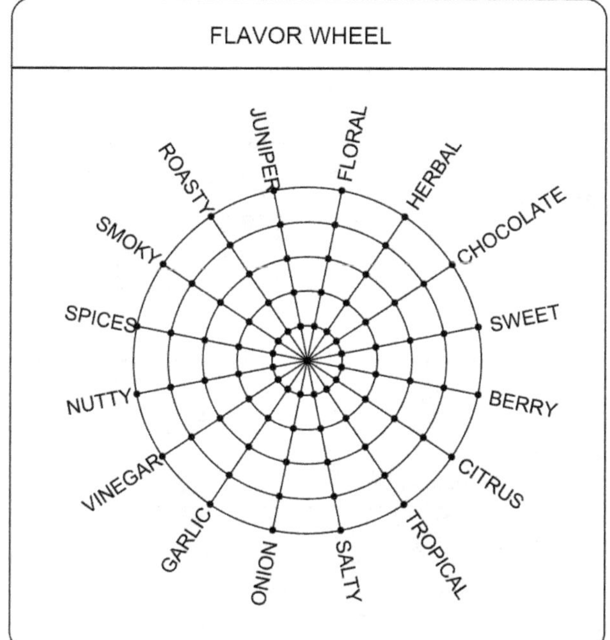

MAIN INGREDIENTS

HEAT METER

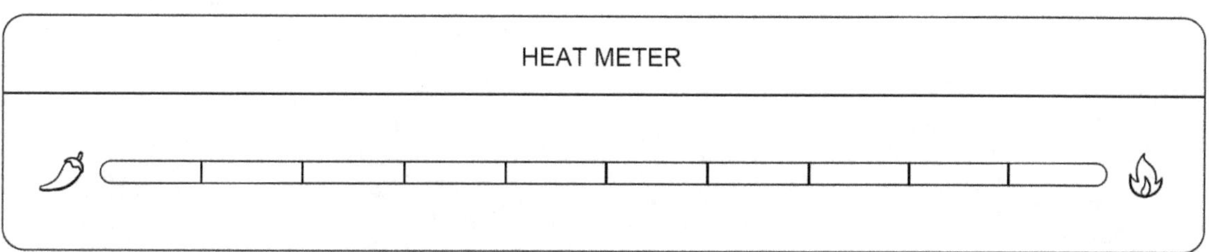

ADDITIONAL NOTES

FINAL RATING

APPEARANCE ☆☆☆☆☆

SMELL ☆☆☆☆☆

TASTE ☆☆☆☆☆

SPICINESS ☆☆☆☆☆

OVERALL RATING ☆☆☆☆☆

NAME	BRAND
ORIGIN	SAMPLED
SCOVILLE	TEXTURE
COLOR	PRICE

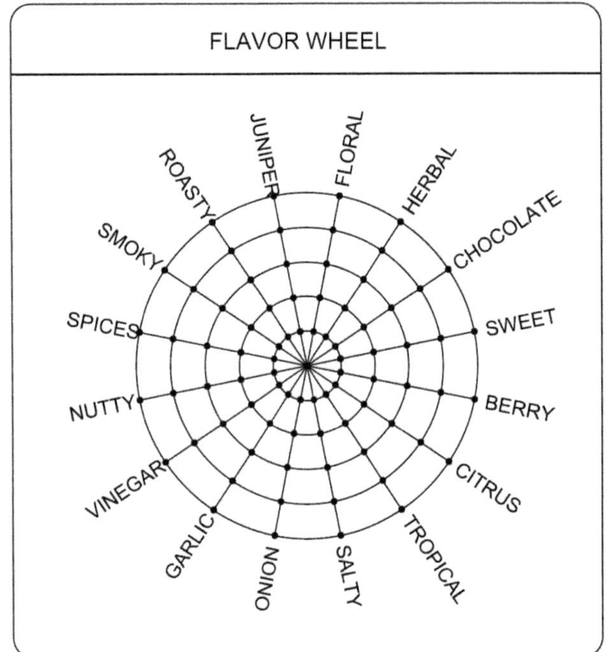

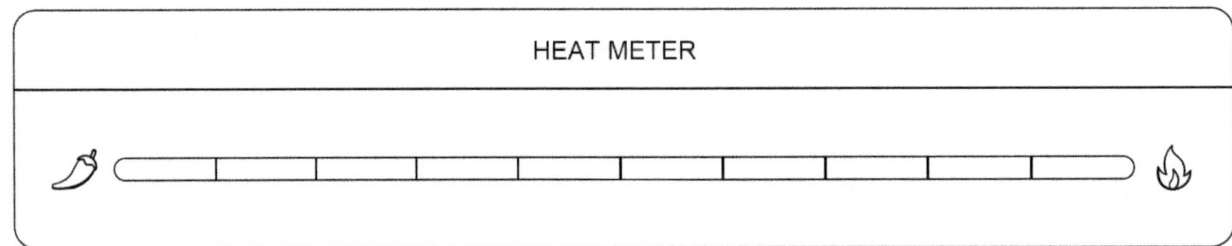

ADDITIONAL NOTES

NAME	BRAND
ORIGIN	SAMPLED
SCOVILLE	TEXTURE
COLOR	PRICE

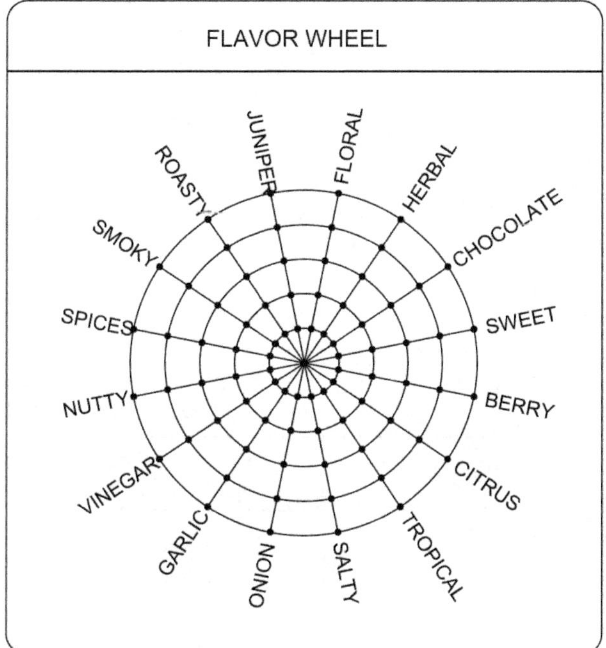

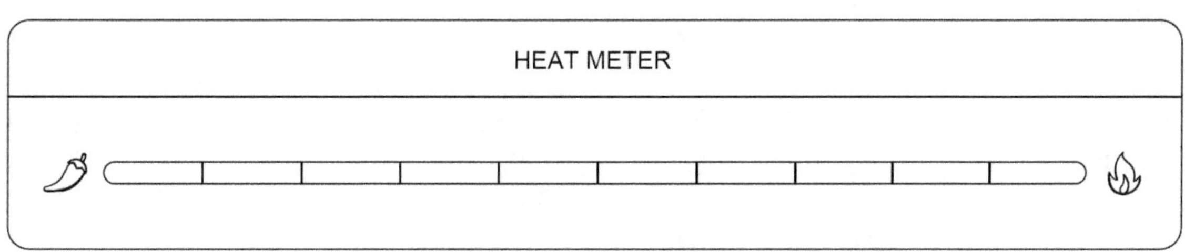

ADDITIONAL NOTES

NAME	BRAND
ORIGIN	SAMPLED
SCOVILLE	TEXTURE
COLOR	PRICE

FLAVOR WHEEL

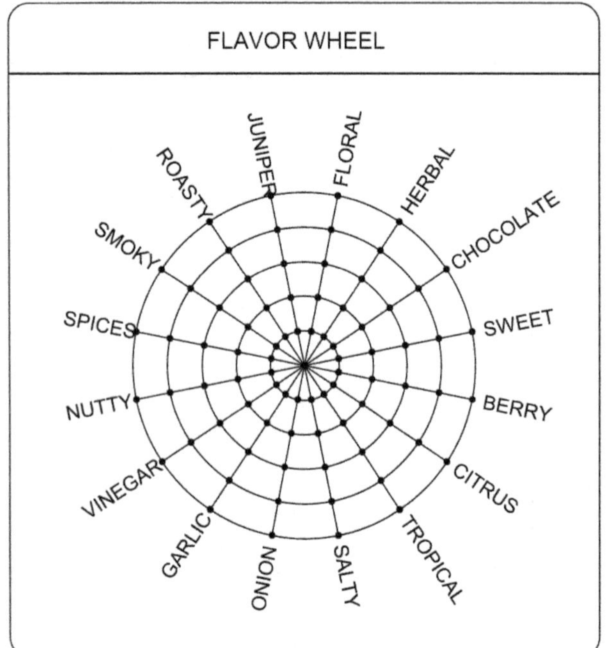

MAIN INGREDIENTS

HEAT METER

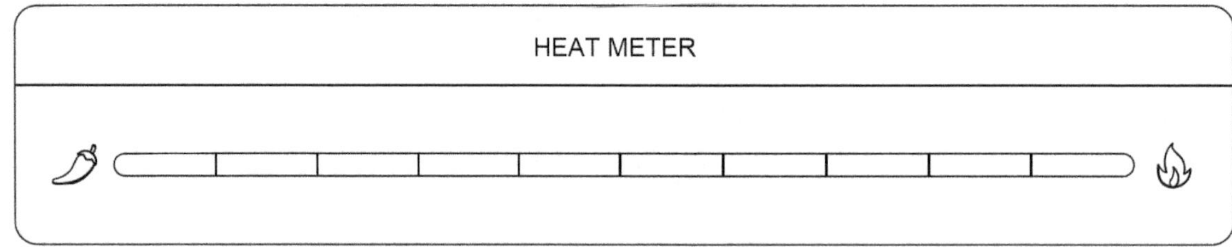

ADDITIONAL NOTES

FINAL RATING

NAME	BRAND
ORIGIN	SAMPLED
SCOVILLE	TEXTURE
COLOR	PRICE

FLAVOR WHEEL

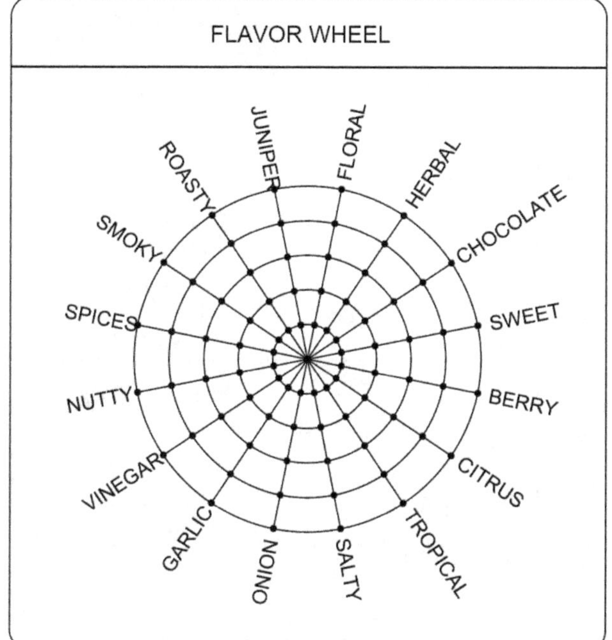

MAIN INGREDIENTS

HEAT METER

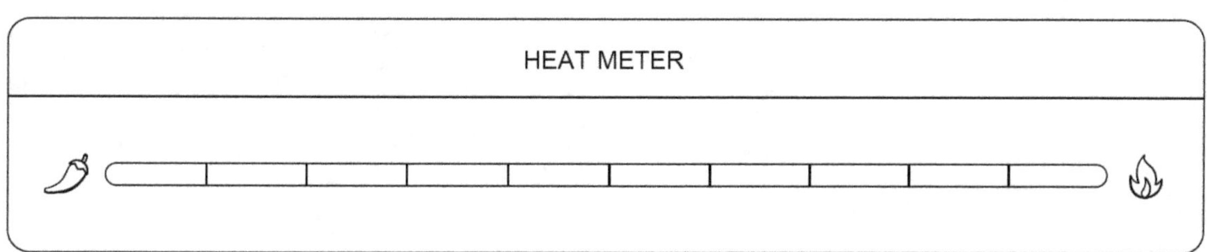

ADDITIONAL NOTES

FINAL RATING

APPEARANCE ☆☆☆☆☆

SMELL ☆☆☆☆☆

TASTE ☆☆☆☆☆

SPICINESS ☆☆☆☆☆

OVERALL RATING ☆☆☆☆☆

NAME	BRAND
ORIGIN	SAMPLED
SCOVILLE	TEXTURE
COLOR	PRICE

FLAVOR WHEEL

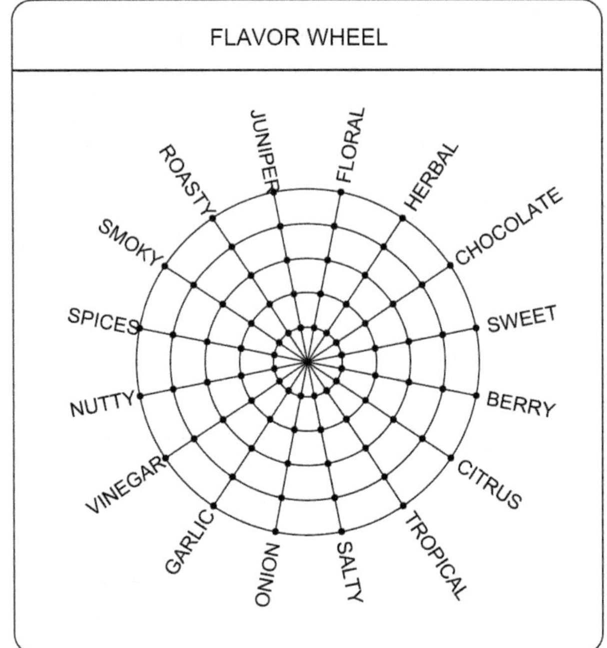

MAIN INGREDIENTS

HEAT METER

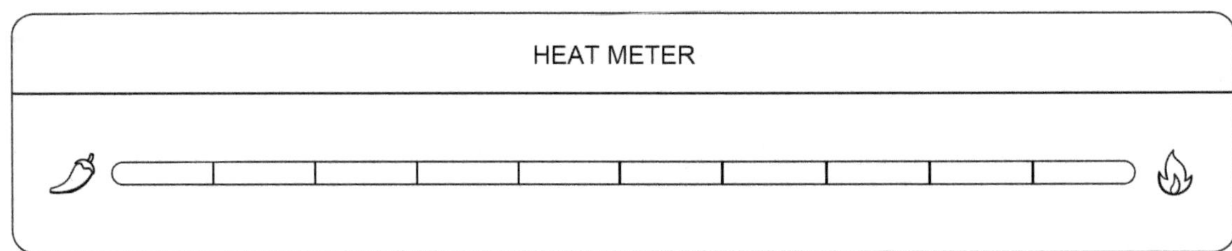

ADDITIONAL NOTES

FINAL RATING

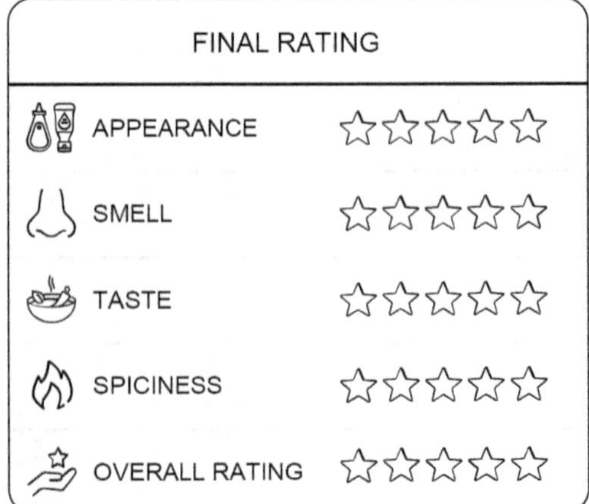

NAME	BRAND
ORIGIN	SAMPLED
SCOVILLE	TEXTURE
COLOR	PRICE

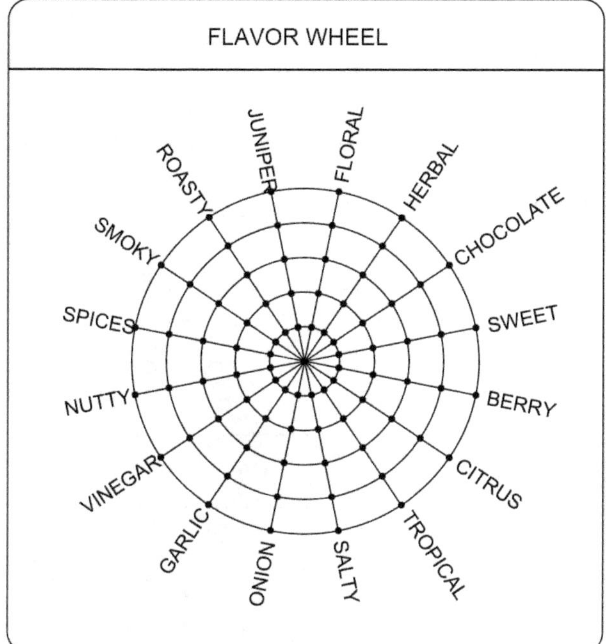

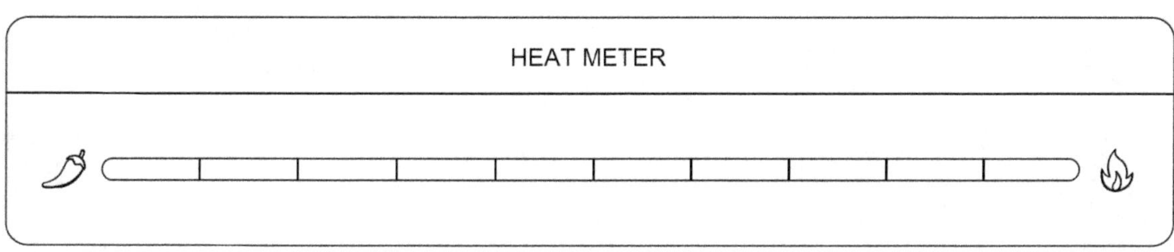

ADDITIONAL NOTES

FINAL RATING	
APPEARANCE	☆☆☆☆☆
SMELL	☆☆☆☆☆
TASTE	☆☆☆☆☆
SPICINESS	☆☆☆☆☆
OVERALL RATING	☆☆☆☆☆

NAME	BRAND
ORIGIN	SAMPLED
SCOVILLE	TEXTURE
COLOR	PRICE

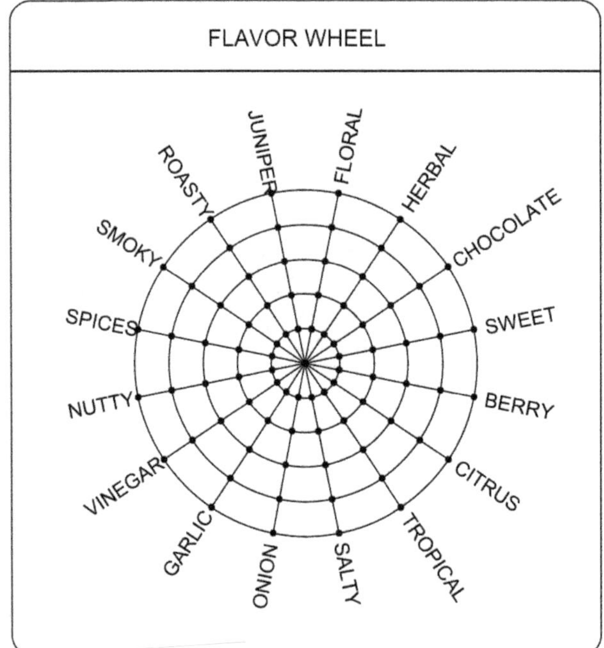

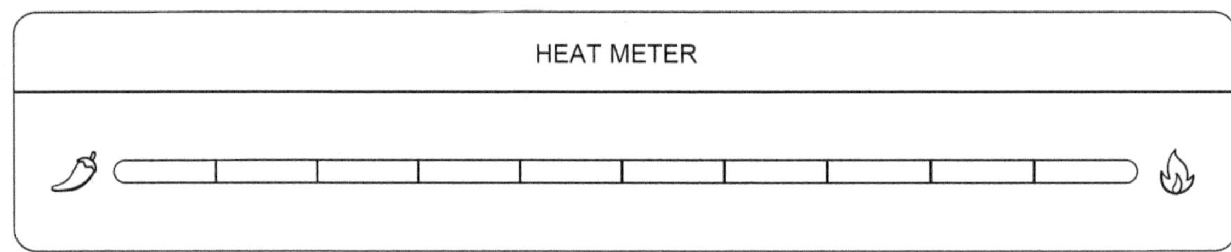

ADDITIONAL NOTES

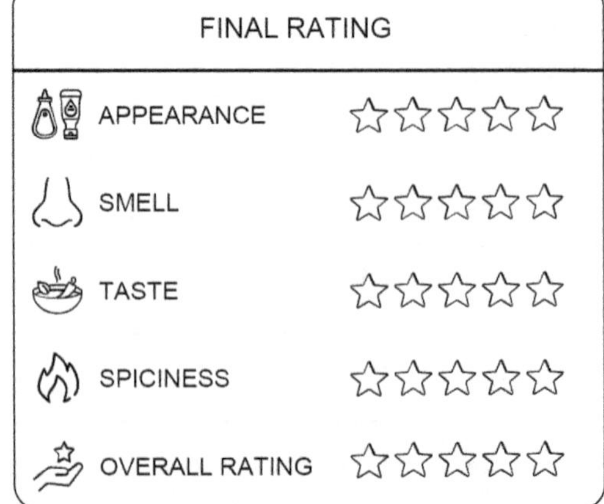

NAME	BRAND
ORIGIN	SAMPLED
SCOVILLE	TEXTURE
COLOR	PRICE

FLAVOR WHEEL

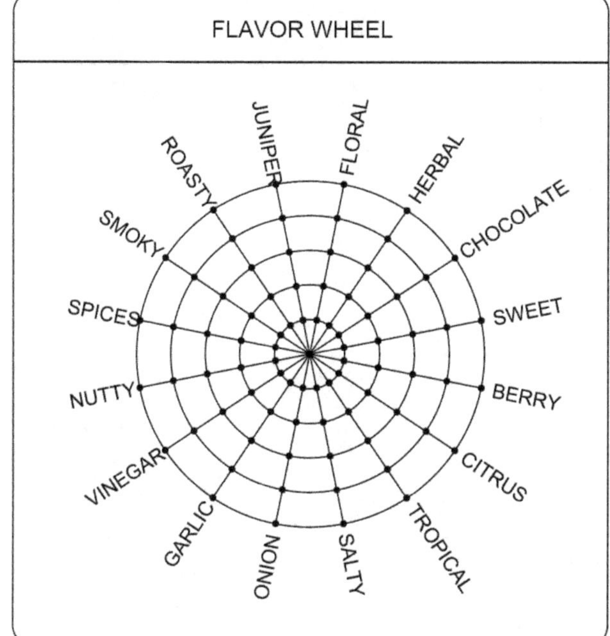

MAIN INGREDIENTS

HEAT METER

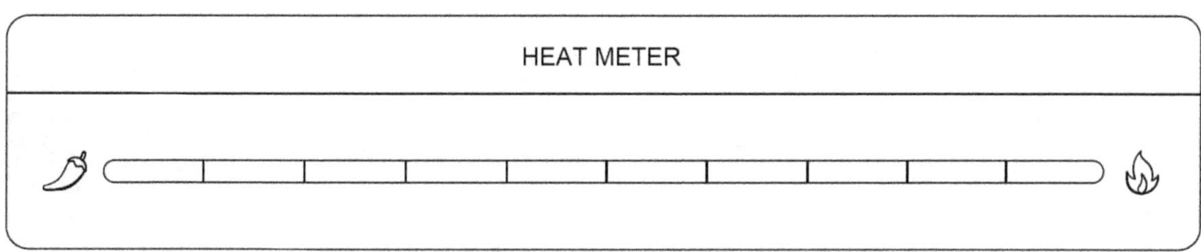

ADDITIONAL NOTES

FINAL RATING

- APPEARANCE ☆☆☆☆☆
- SMELL ☆☆☆☆☆
- TASTE ☆☆☆☆☆
- SPICINESS ☆☆☆☆☆
- OVERALL RATING ☆☆☆☆☆

NAME	BRAND
ORIGIN	SAMPLED
SCOVILLE	TEXTURE
COLOR	PRICE

FLAVOR WHEEL

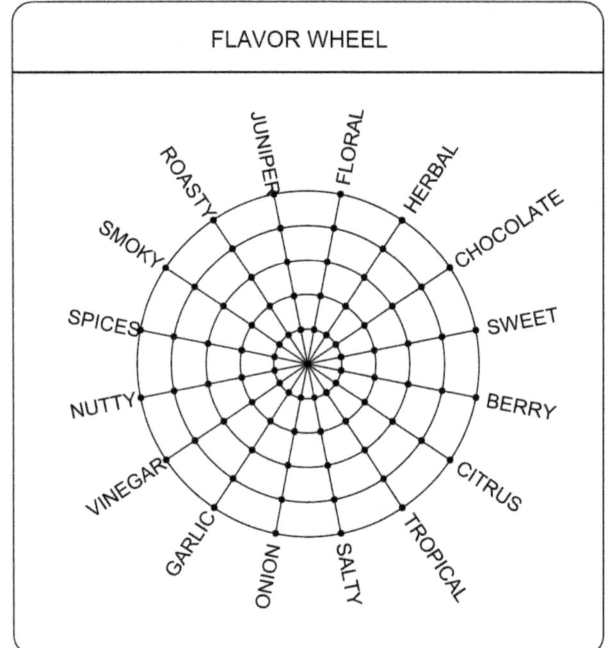

MAIN INGREDIENTS

HEAT METER

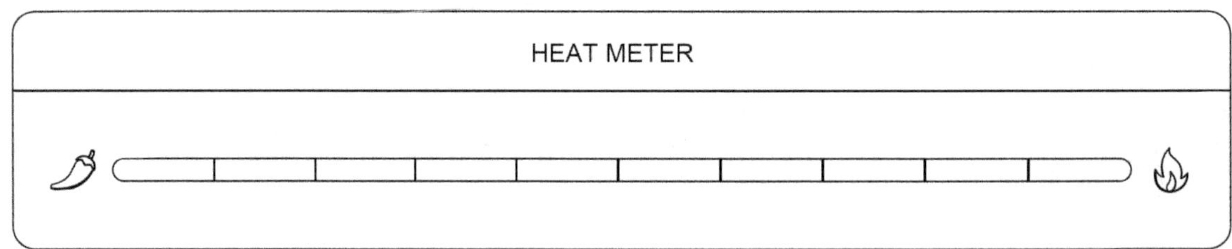

ADDITIONAL NOTES

FINAL RATING

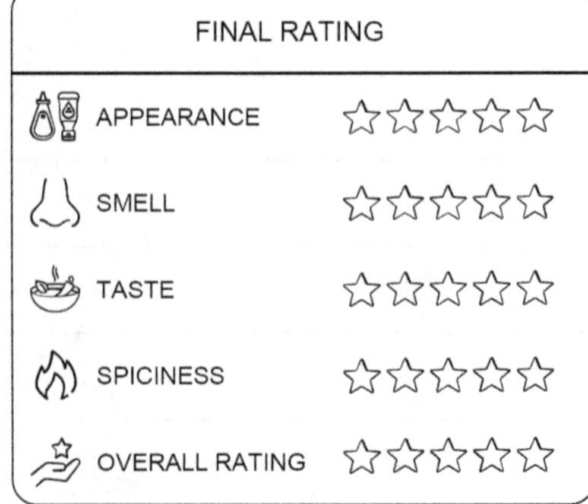

NAME	BRAND
ORIGIN	SAMPLED
SCOVILLE	TEXTURE
COLOR	PRICE

FLAVOR WHEEL

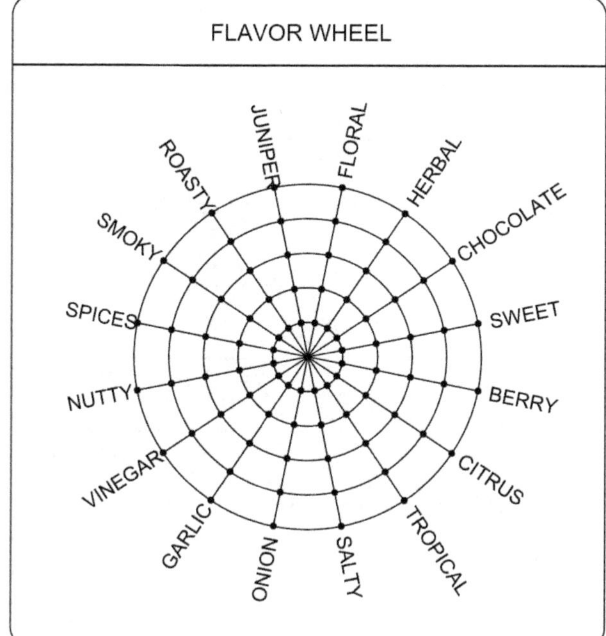

MAIN INGREDIENTS

HEAT METER

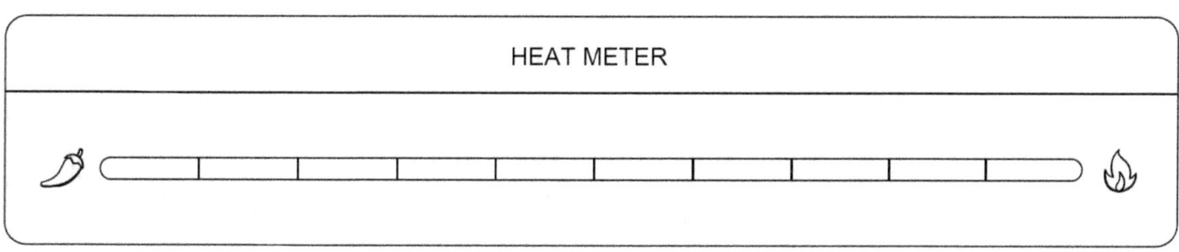

ADDITIONAL NOTES

FINAL RATING

- APPEARANCE ☆☆☆☆☆
- SMELL ☆☆☆☆☆
- TASTE ☆☆☆☆☆
- SPICINESS ☆☆☆☆☆
- OVERALL RATING ☆☆☆☆☆

NAME	BRAND
ORIGIN	SAMPLED
SCOVILLE	TEXTURE
COLOR	PRICE

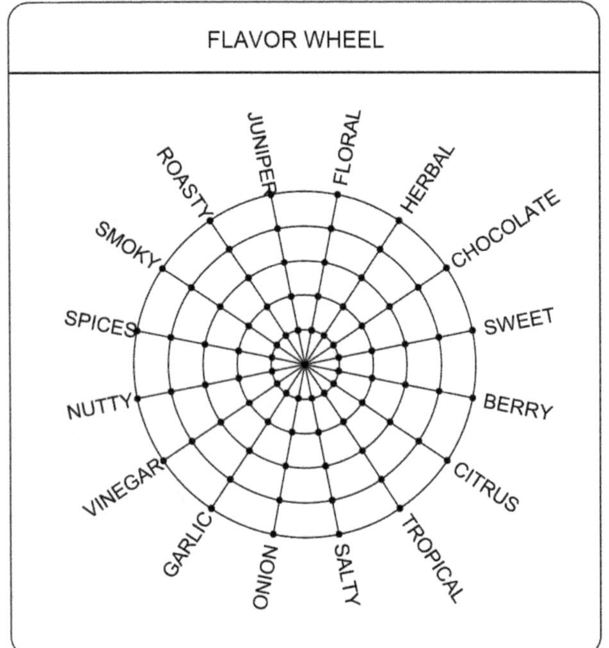

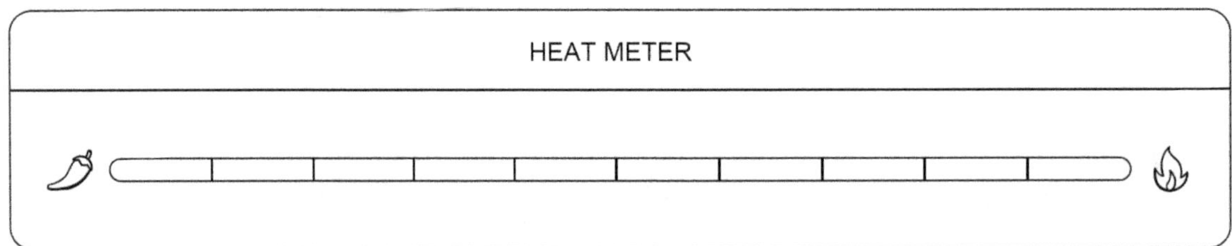

ADDITIONAL NOTES

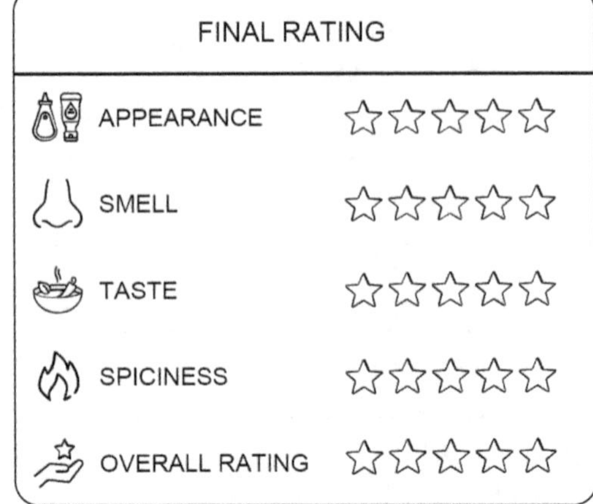

NAME	BRAND
ORIGIN	SAMPLED
SCOVILLE	TEXTURE
COLOR	PRICE

FLAVOR WHEEL

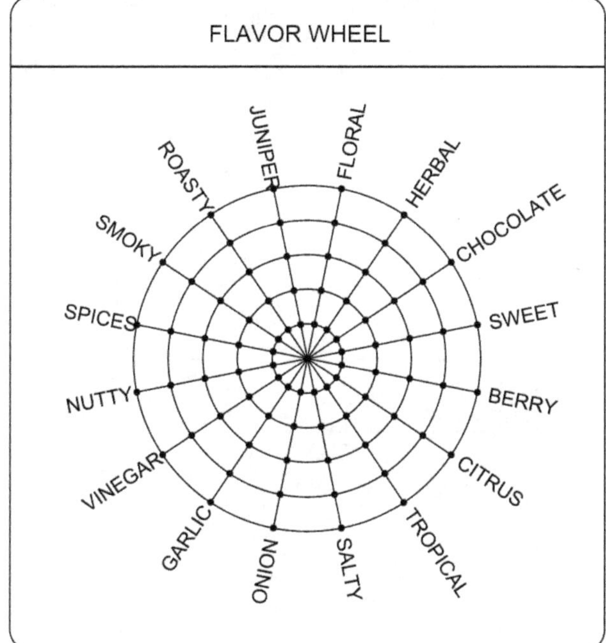

MAIN INGREDIENTS

HEAT METER

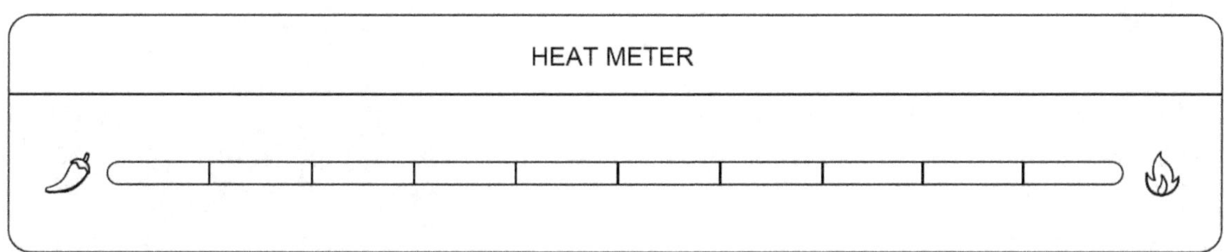

ADDITIONAL NOTES

FINAL RATING

APPEARANCE ☆☆☆☆☆

SMELL ☆☆☆☆☆

TASTE ☆☆☆☆☆

SPICINESS ☆☆☆☆☆

OVERALL RATING ☆☆☆☆☆

NAME	BRAND
ORIGIN	SAMPLED
SCOVILLE	TEXTURE
COLOR	PRICE

FLAVOR WHEEL

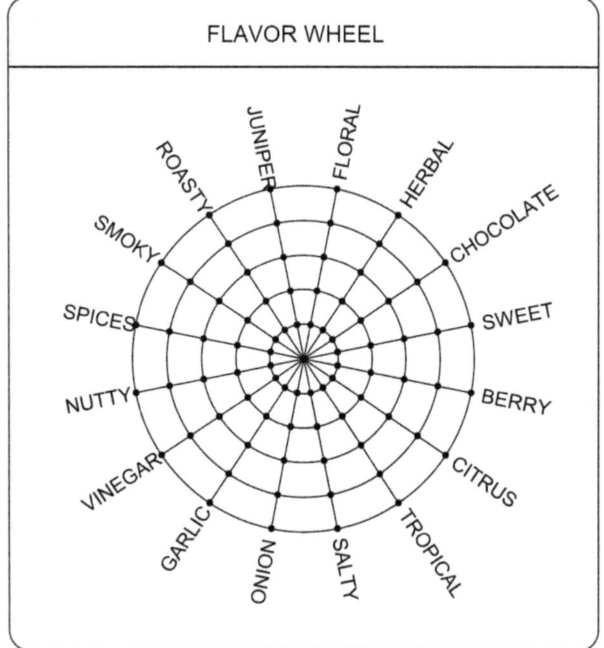

MAIN INGREDIENTS

HEAT METER

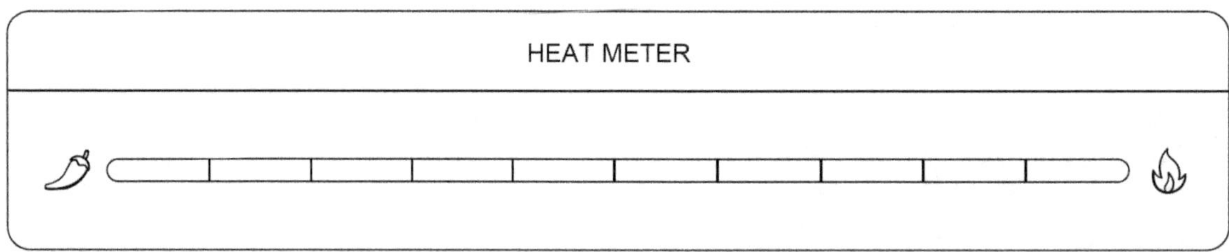

ADDITIONAL NOTES

FINAL RATING

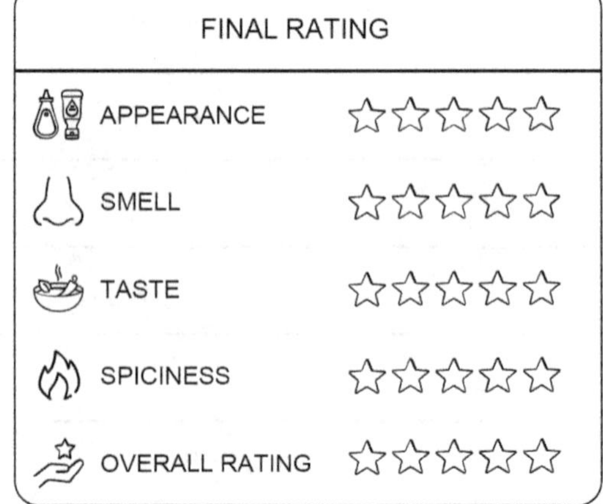

NAME	BRAND
ORIGIN	SAMPLED
SCOVILLE	TEXTURE
COLOR	PRICE

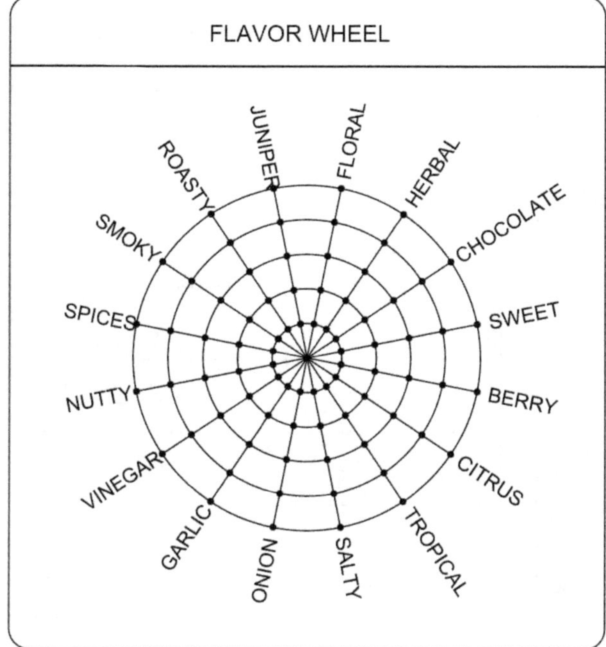

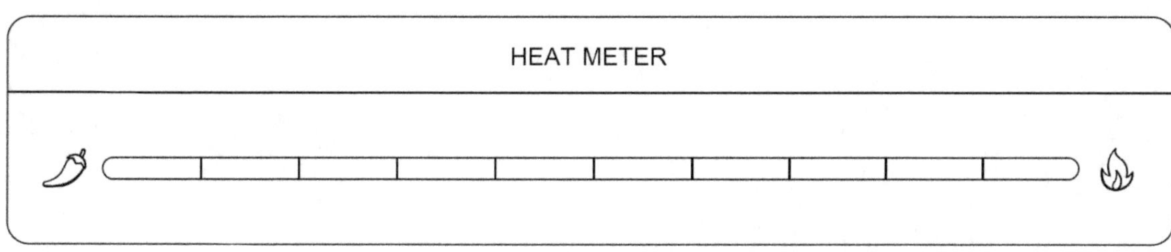

ADDITIONAL NOTES

FINAL RATING

APPEARANCE ☆☆☆☆☆

SMELL ☆☆☆☆☆

TASTE ☆☆☆☆☆

SPICINESS ☆☆☆☆☆

OVERALL RATING ☆☆☆☆☆

NAME	BRAND
ORIGIN	SAMPLED
SCOVILLE	TEXTURE
COLOR	PRICE

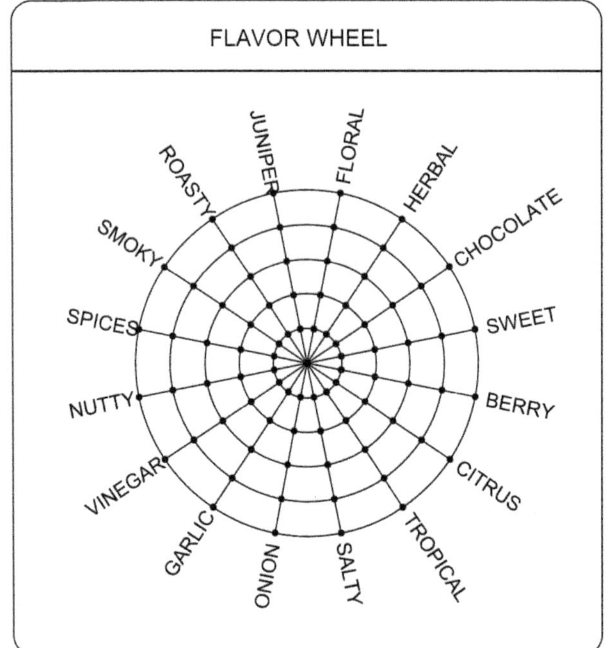

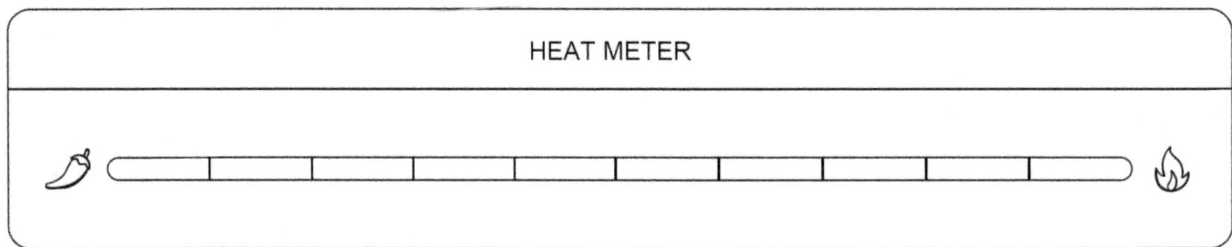

ADDITIONAL NOTES

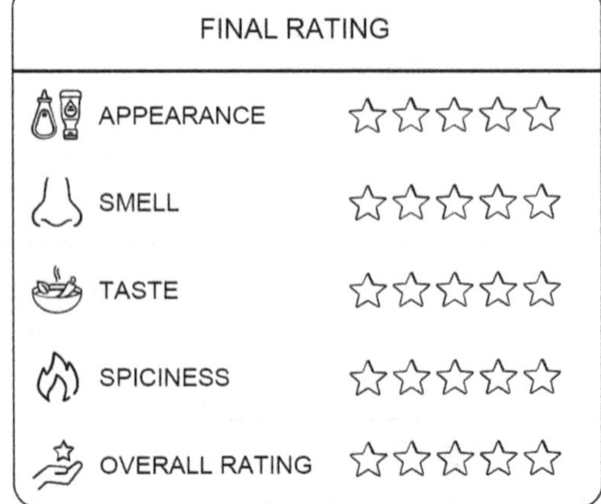

NAME	BRAND
ORIGIN	SAMPLED
SCOVILLE	TEXTURE
COLOR	PRICE

FLAVOR WHEEL

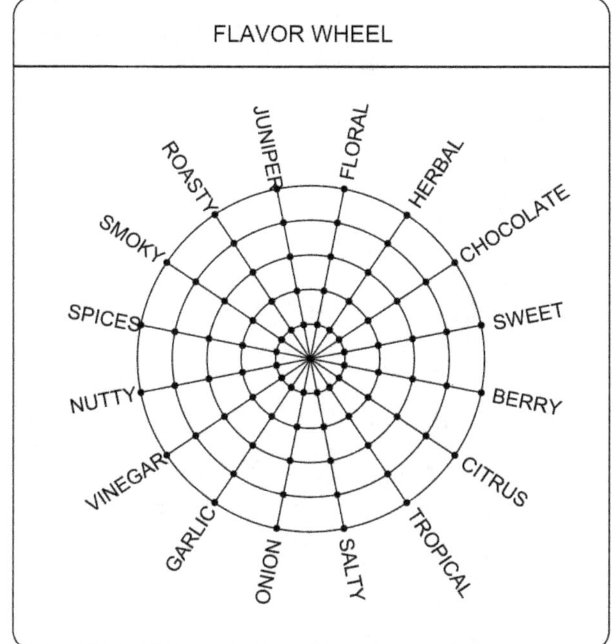

MAIN INGREDIENTS

HEAT METER

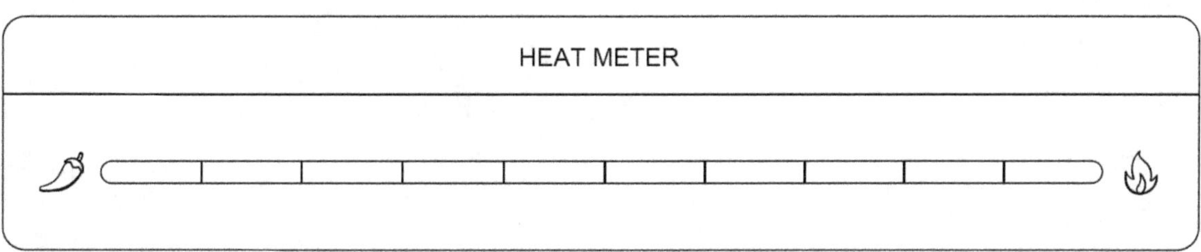

ADDITIONAL NOTES

FINAL RATING

APPEARANCE ☆☆☆☆☆

SMELL ☆☆☆☆☆

TASTE ☆☆☆☆☆

SPICINESS ☆☆☆☆☆

OVERALL RATING ☆☆☆☆☆

NAME	BRAND
ORIGIN	SAMPLED
SCOVILLE	TEXTURE
COLOR	PRICE

FLAVOR WHEEL

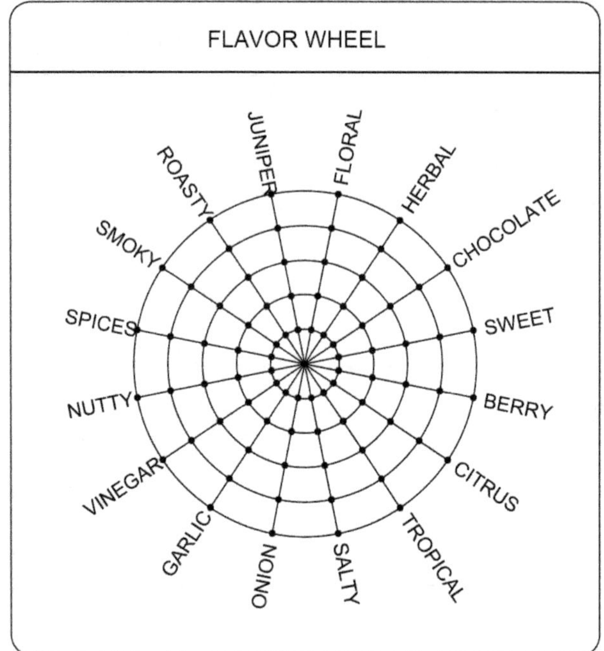

MAIN INGREDIENTS

HEAT METER

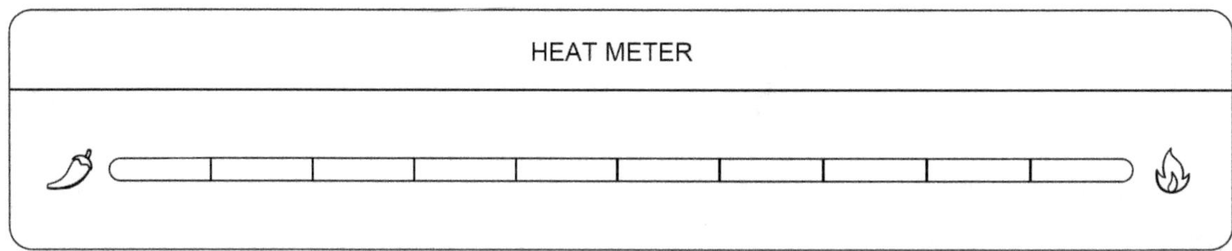

ADDITIONAL NOTES

FINAL RATING

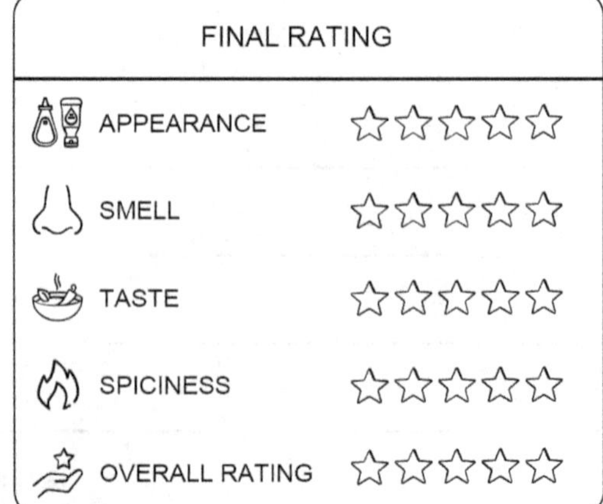

NAME	BRAND
ORIGIN	SAMPLED
SCOVILLE	TEXTURE
COLOR	PRICE

FLAVOR WHEEL

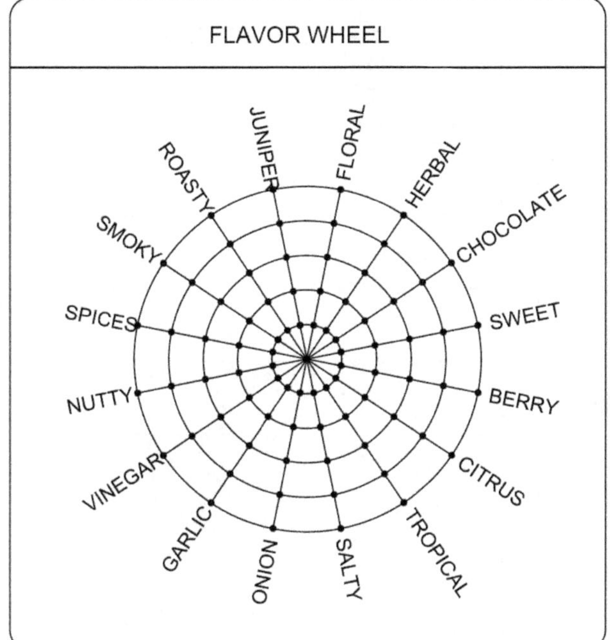

MAIN INGREDIENTS

HEAT METER

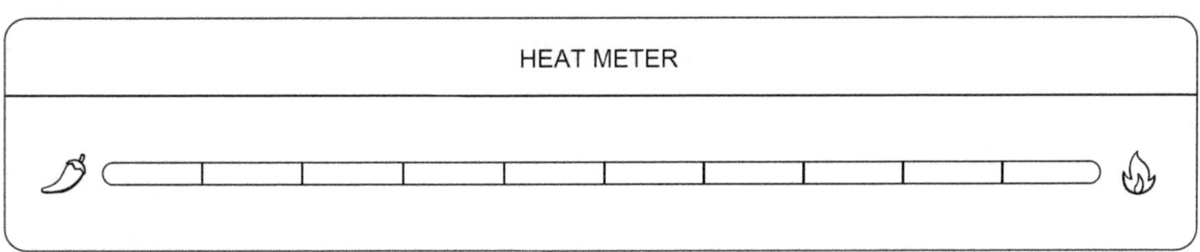

ADDITIONAL NOTES

FINAL RATING

APPEARANCE ☆☆☆☆☆

SMELL ☆☆☆☆☆

TASTE ☆☆☆☆☆

SPICINESS ☆☆☆☆☆

OVERALL RATING ☆☆☆☆☆

NAME	BRAND
ORIGIN	SAMPLED
SCOVILLE	TEXTURE
COLOR	PRICE

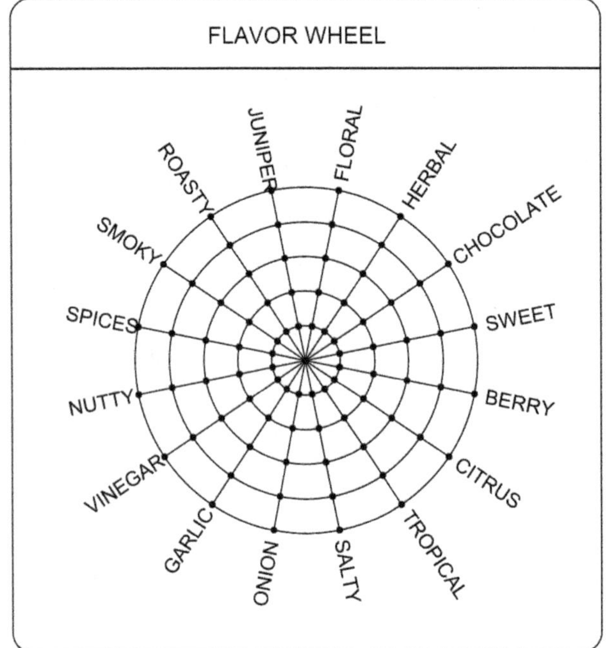

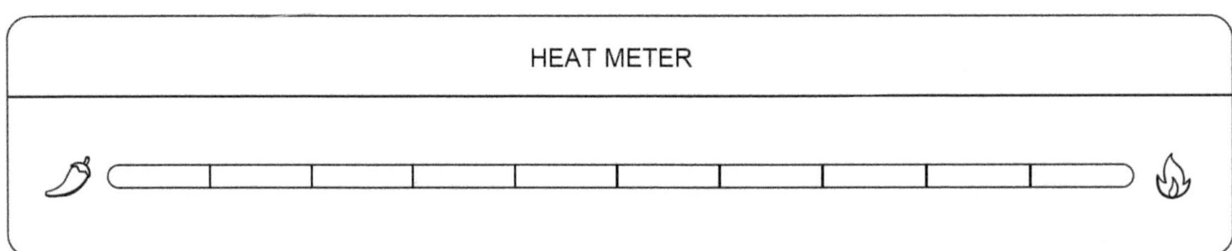

ADDITIONAL NOTES

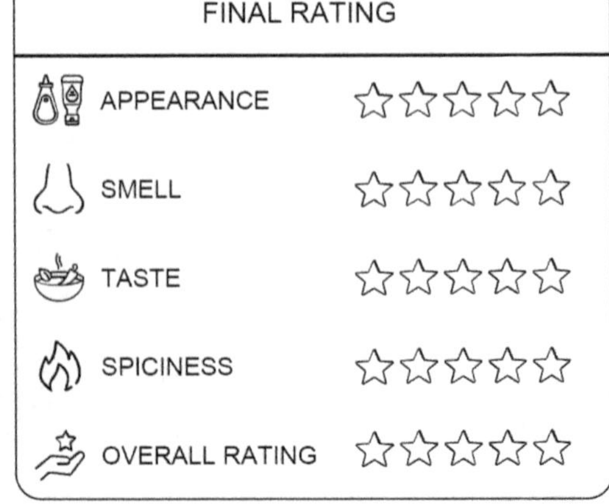

NAME	BRAND
ORIGIN	SAMPLED
SCOVILLE	TEXTURE
COLOR	PRICE

FLAVOR WHEEL

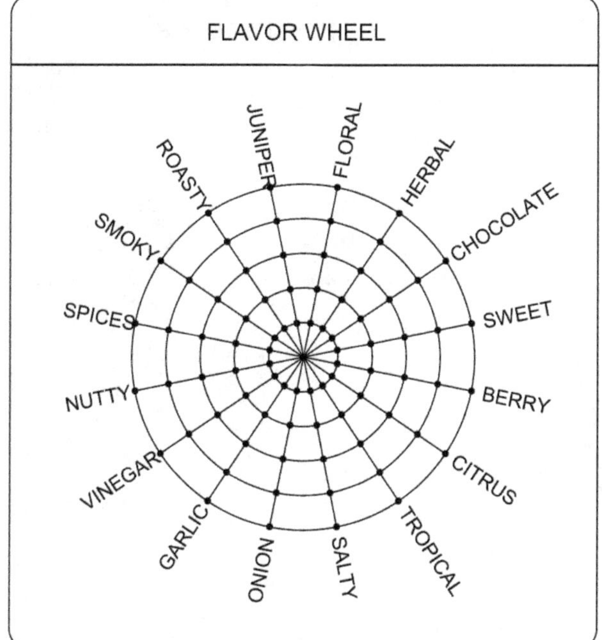

MAIN INGREDIENTS

HEAT METER

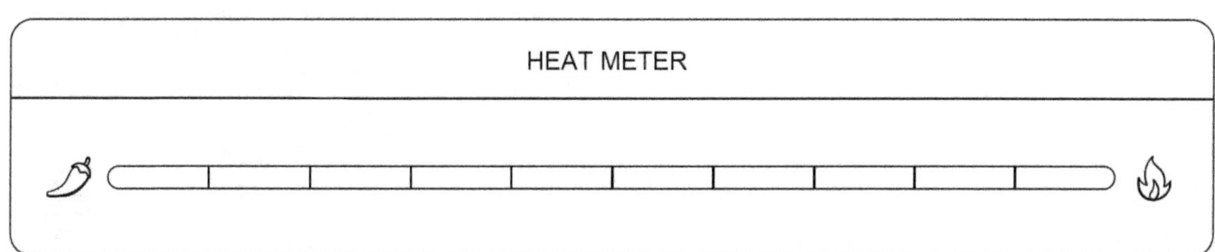

ADDITIONAL NOTES

FINAL RATING

APPEARANCE ☆☆☆☆☆

SMELL ☆☆☆☆☆

TASTE ☆☆☆☆☆

SPICINESS ☆☆☆☆☆

OVERALL RATING ☆☆☆☆☆

NAME	BRAND
ORIGIN	SAMPLED
SCOVILLE	TEXTURE
COLOR	PRICE

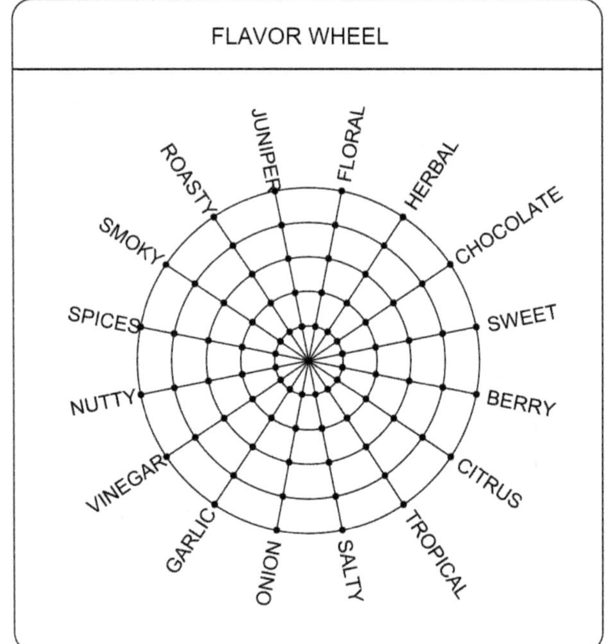

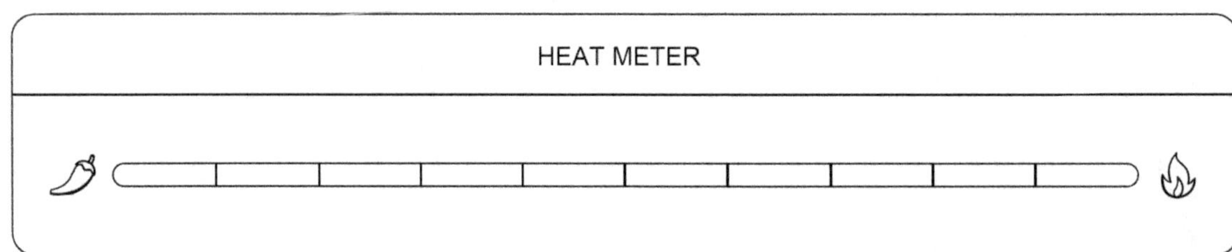

ADDITIONAL NOTES

NAME	BRAND
ORIGIN	SAMPLED
SCOVILLE	TEXTURE
COLOR	PRICE

FLAVOR WHEEL

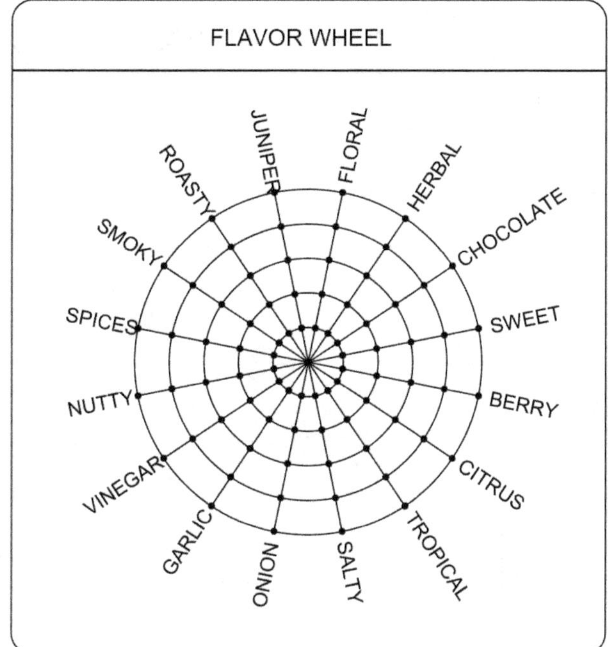

MAIN INGREDIENTS

HEAT METER

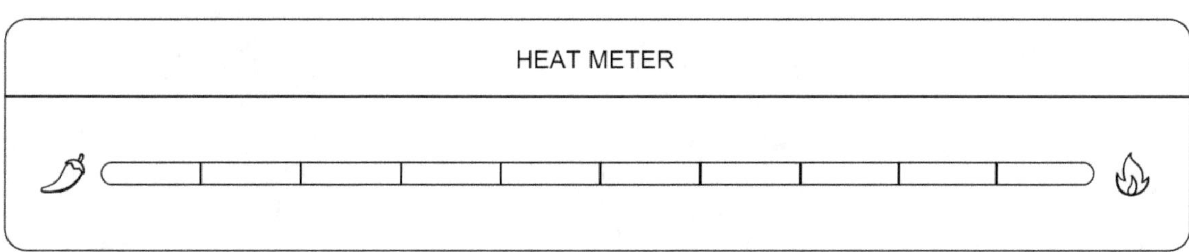

ADDITIONAL NOTES

FINAL RATING

APPEARANCE ☆☆☆☆☆

SMELL ☆☆☆☆☆

TASTE ☆☆☆☆☆

SPICINESS ☆☆☆☆☆

OVERALL RATING ☆☆☆☆☆

NAME	BRAND
ORIGIN	SAMPLED
SCOVILLE	TEXTURE
COLOR	PRICE

FLAVOR WHEEL

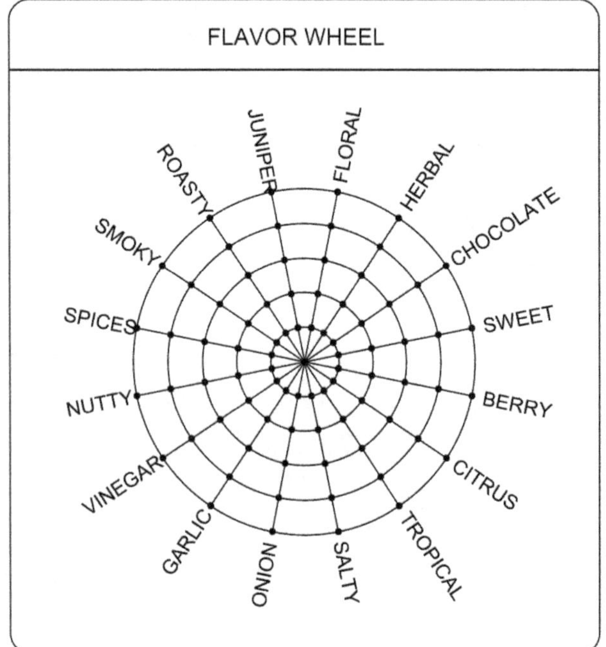

MAIN INGREDIENTS

HEAT METER

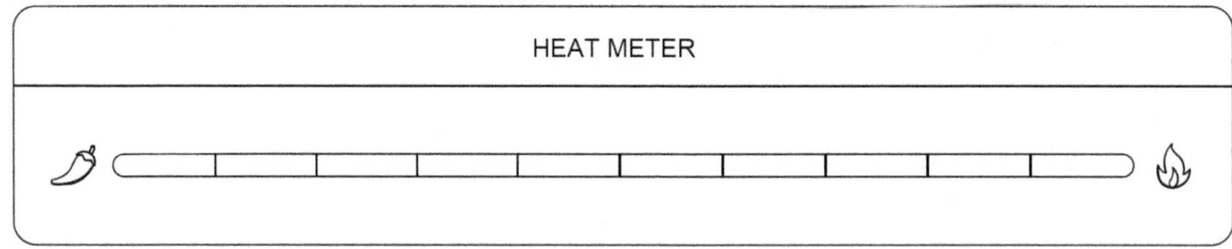

ADDITIONAL NOTES

FINAL RATING

NAME	BRAND
ORIGIN	SAMPLED
SCOVILLE	TEXTURE
COLOR	PRICE

FLAVOR WHEEL

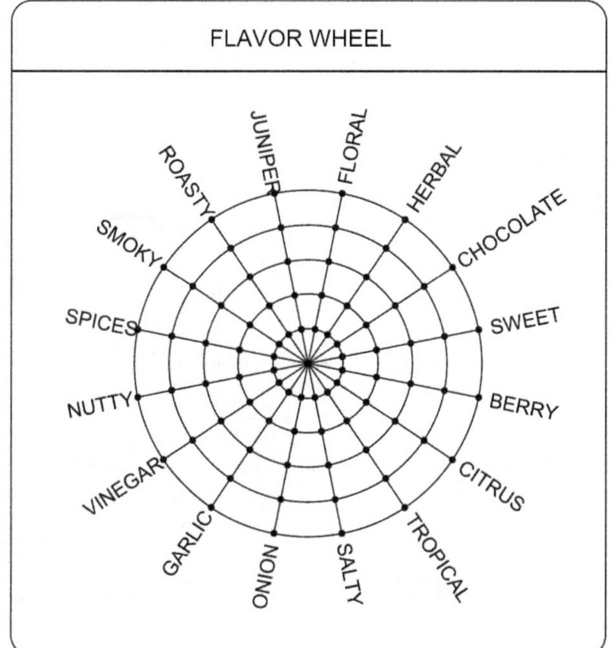

MAIN INGREDIENTS

HEAT METER

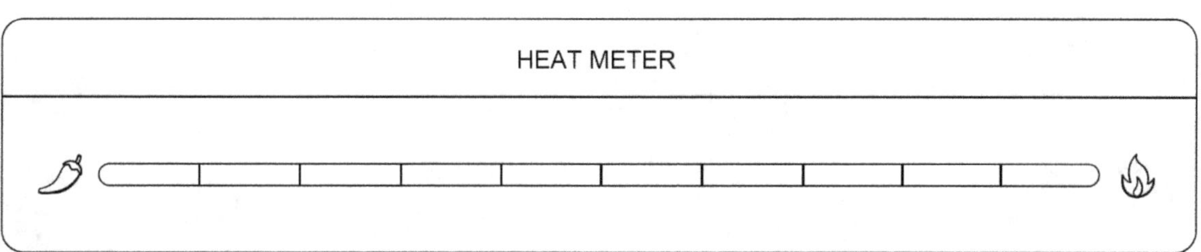

ADDITIONAL NOTES

FINAL RATING

APPEARANCE	☆☆☆☆☆
SMELL	☆☆☆☆☆
TASTE	☆☆☆☆☆
SPICINESS	☆☆☆☆☆
OVERALL RATING	☆☆☆☆☆

NAME	BRAND
ORIGIN	SAMPLED
SCOVILLE	TEXTURE
COLOR	PRICE

FLAVOR WHEEL

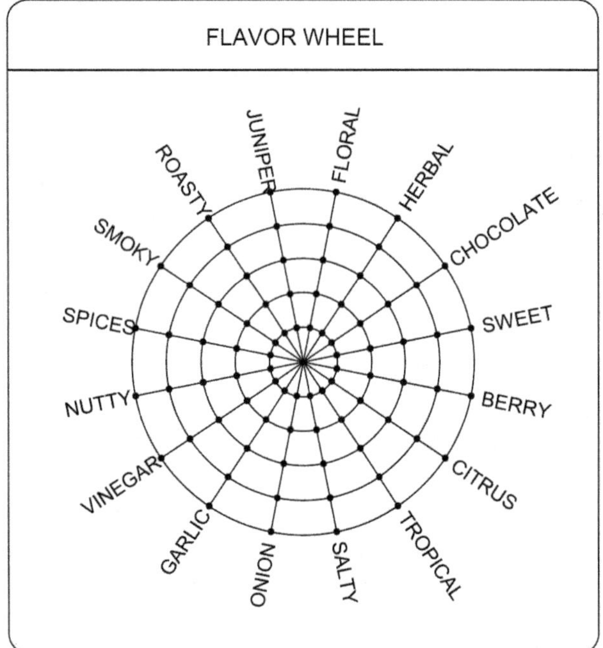

MAIN INGREDIENTS

HEAT METER

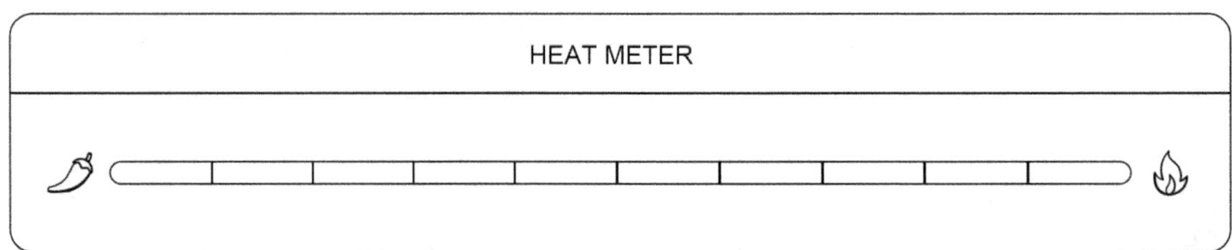

ADDITIONAL NOTES

FINAL RATING

NAME	BRAND
ORIGIN	SAMPLED
SCOVILLE	TEXTURE
COLOR	PRICE

FLAVOR WHEEL

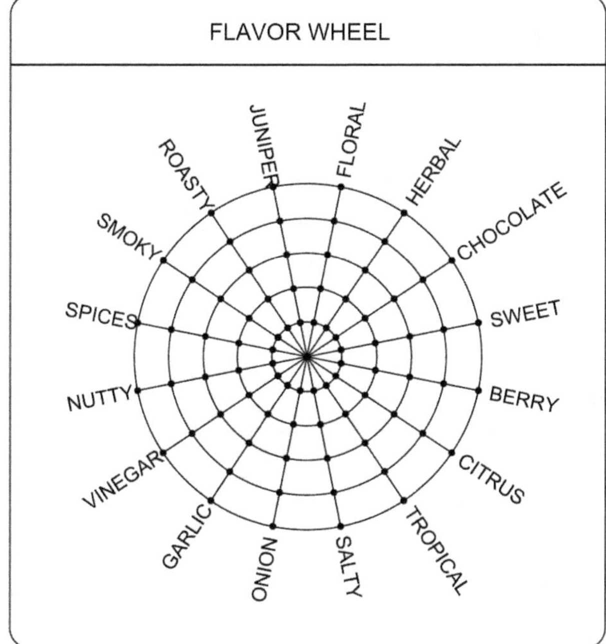

MAIN INGREDIENTS

HEAT METER

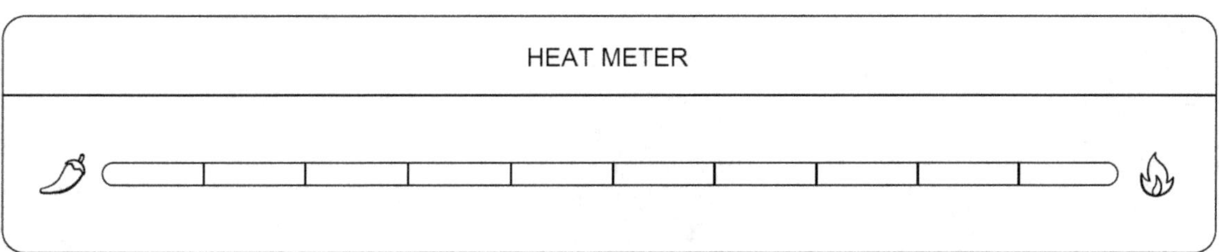

ADDITIONAL NOTES

FINAL RATING

APPEARANCE ☆☆☆☆☆

SMELL ☆☆☆☆☆

TASTE ☆☆☆☆☆

SPICINESS ☆☆☆☆☆

OVERALL RATING ☆☆☆☆☆

NAME	BRAND
ORIGIN	SAMPLED
SCOVILLE	TEXTURE
COLOR	PRICE

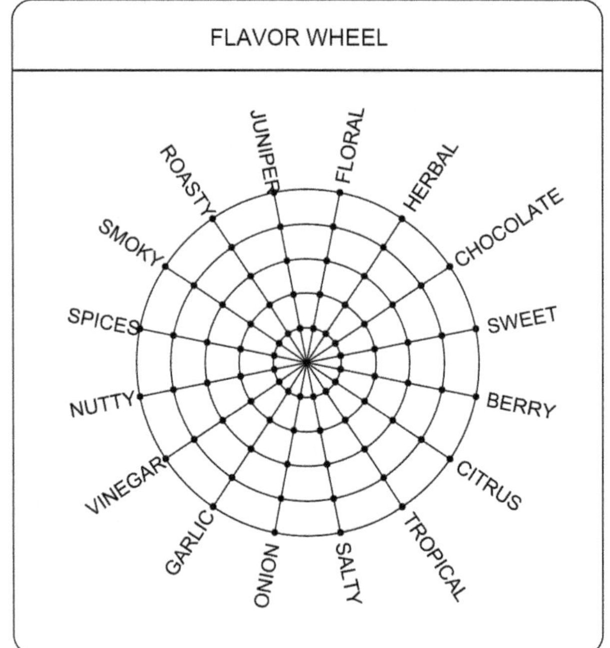

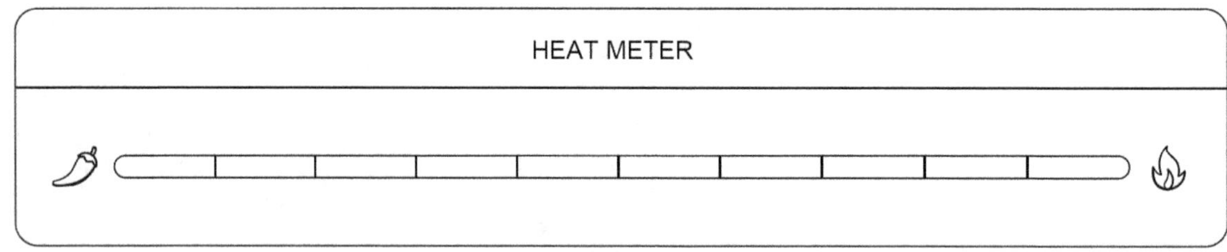

ADDITIONAL NOTES

NAME	BRAND
ORIGIN	SAMPLED
SCOVILLE	TEXTURE
COLOR	PRICE

FLAVOR WHEEL

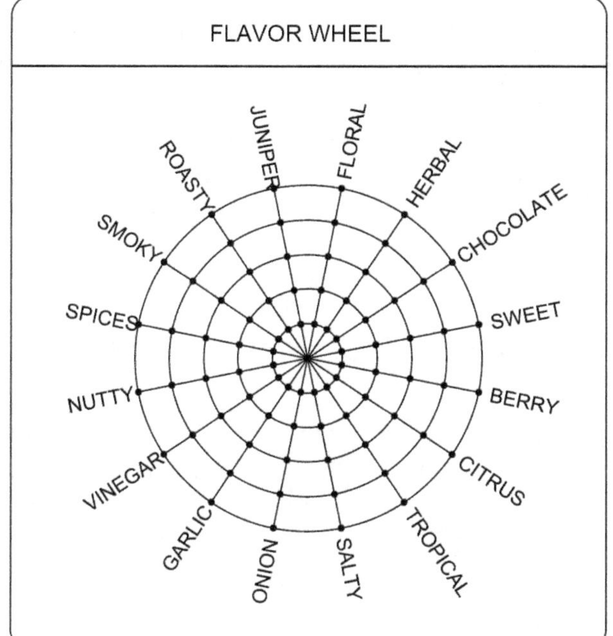

MAIN INGREDIENTS

HEAT METER

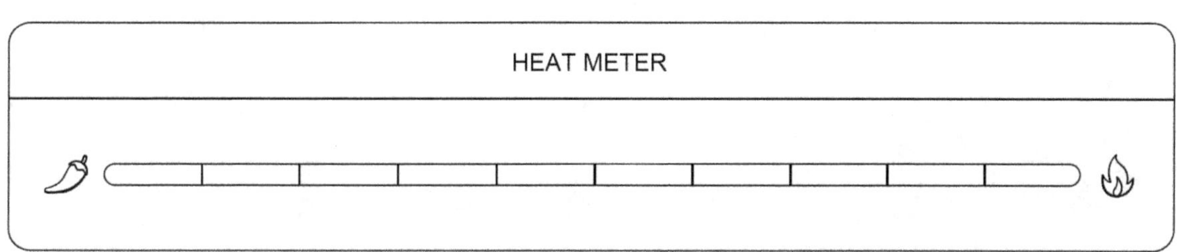

ADDITIONAL NOTES

FINAL RATING

APPEARANCE ☆☆☆☆☆

SMELL ☆☆☆☆☆

TASTE ☆☆☆☆☆

SPICINESS ☆☆☆☆☆

OVERALL RATING ☆☆☆☆☆

NAME	BRAND
ORIGIN	SAMPLED
SCOVILLE	TEXTURE
COLOR	PRICE

FLAVOR WHEEL

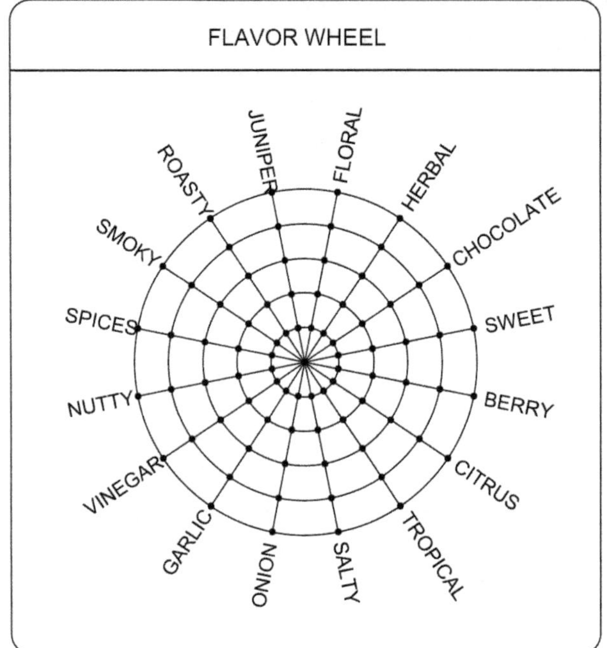

MAIN INGREDIENTS

HEAT METER

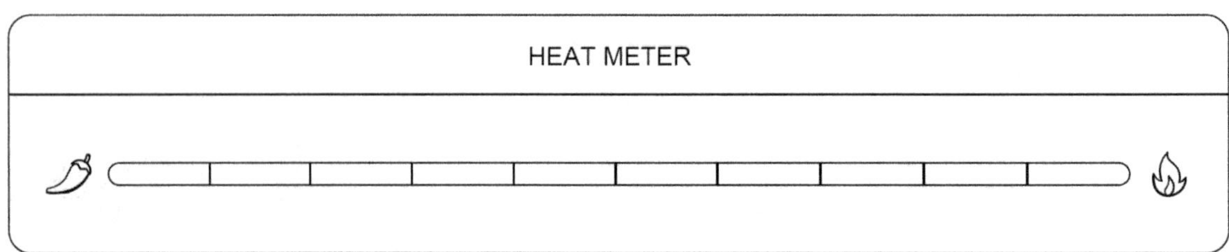

ADDITIONAL NOTES

FINAL RATING

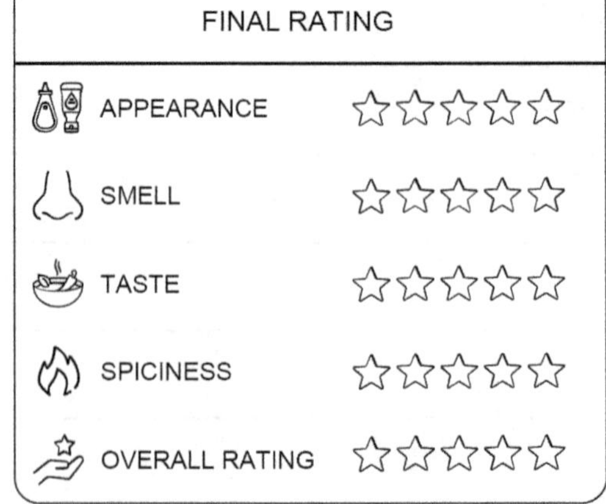

NAME	BRAND
ORIGIN	SAMPLED
SCOVILLE	TEXTURE
COLOR	PRICE

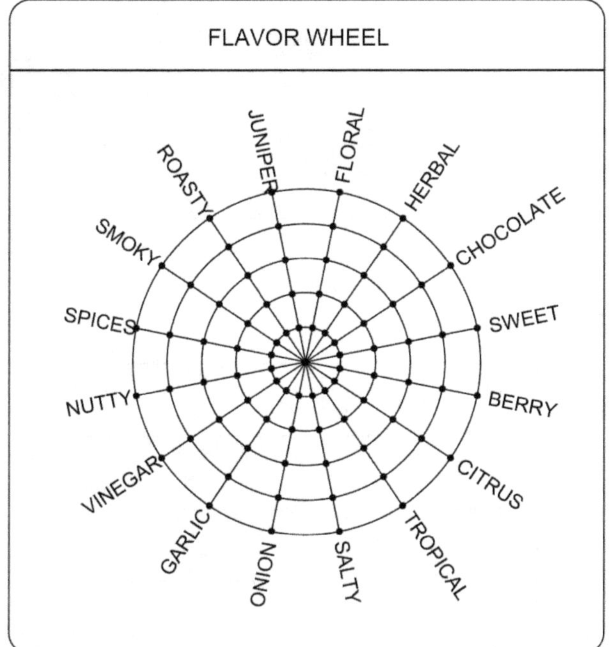

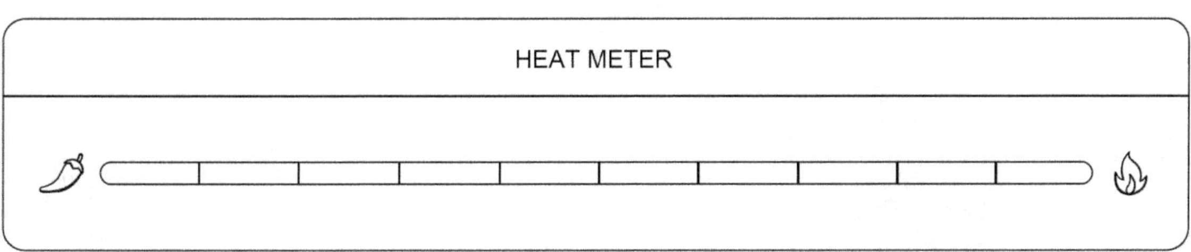

ADDITIONAL NOTES

FINAL RATING

APPEARANCE ☆☆☆☆☆

SMELL ☆☆☆☆☆

TASTE ☆☆☆☆☆

SPICINESS ☆☆☆☆☆

OVERALL RATING ☆☆☆☆☆

NAME	BRAND
ORIGIN	SAMPLED
SCOVILLE	TEXTURE
COLOR	PRICE

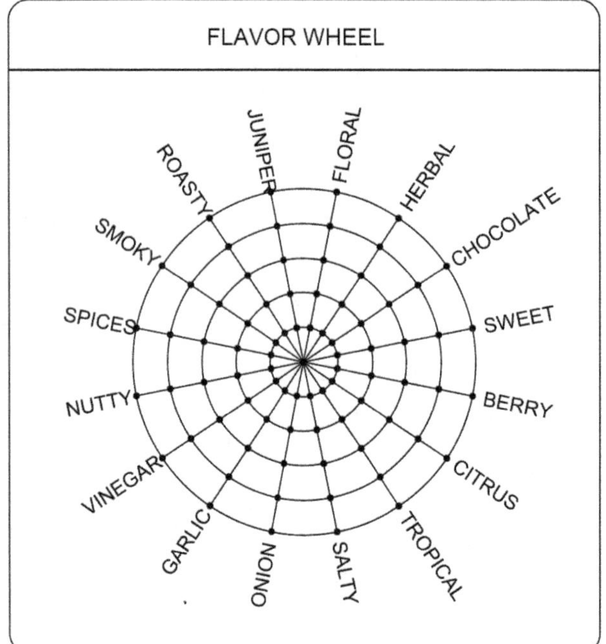

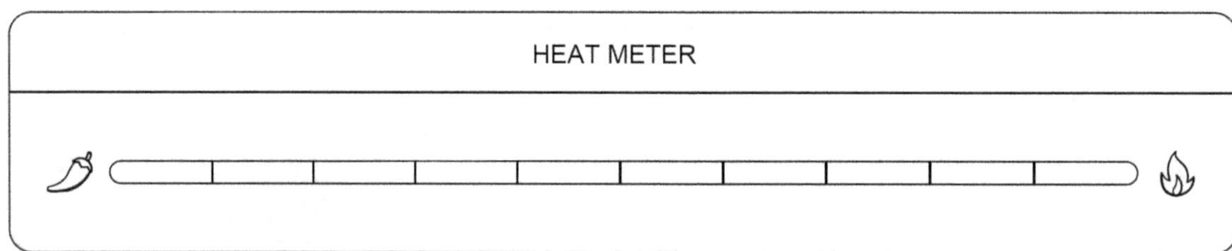

ADDITIONAL NOTES

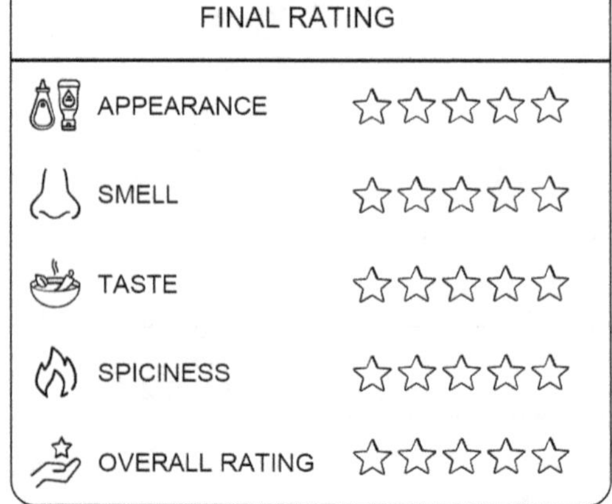

NAME	BRAND
ORIGIN	SAMPLED
SCOVILLE	TEXTURE
COLOR	PRICE

FLAVOR WHEEL

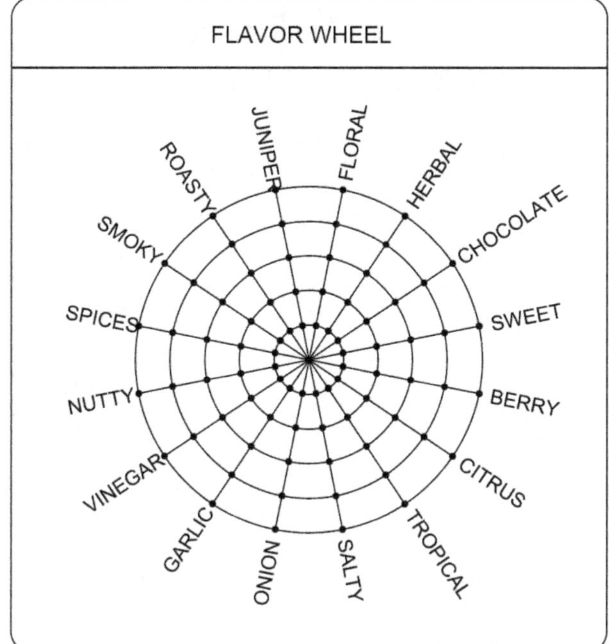

MAIN INGREDIENTS

HEAT METER

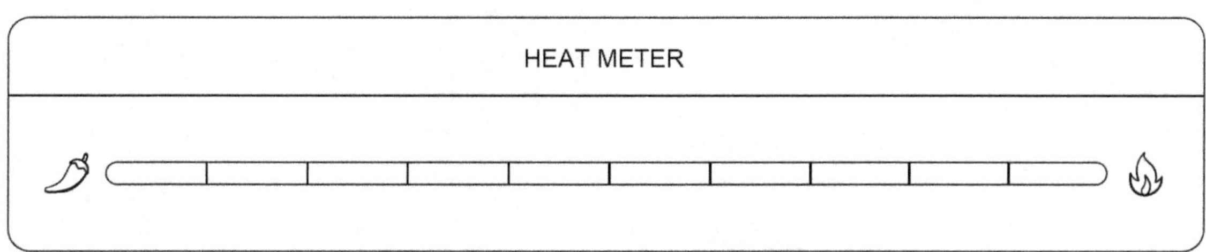

ADDITIONAL NOTES

FINAL RATING

NAME	BRAND
ORIGIN	SAMPLED
SCOVILLE	TEXTURE
COLOR	PRICE

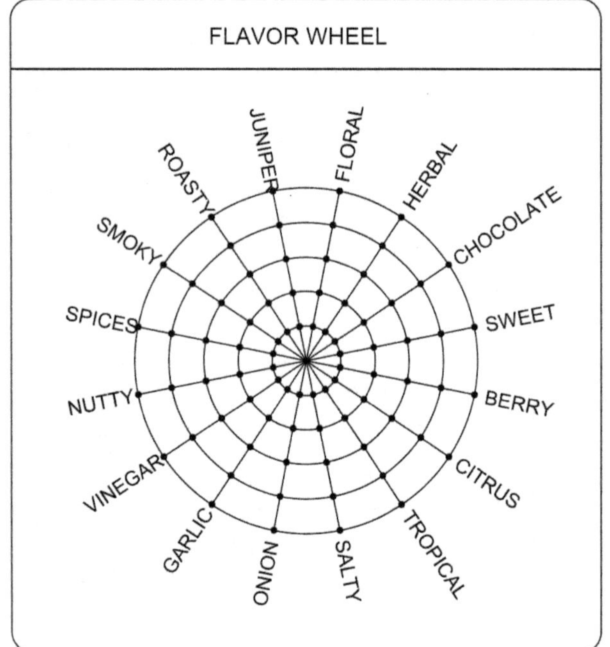

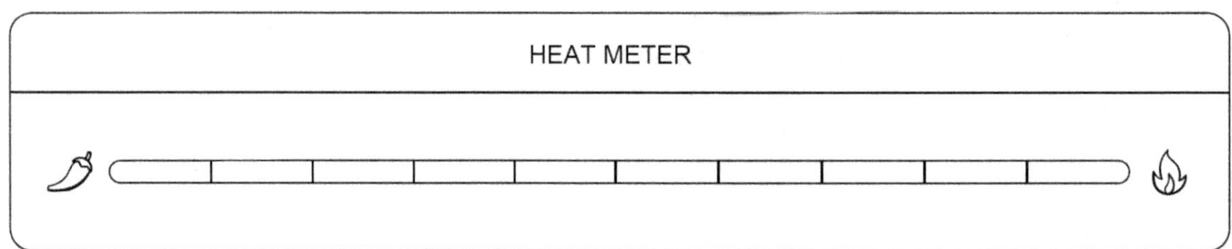

ADDITIONAL NOTES

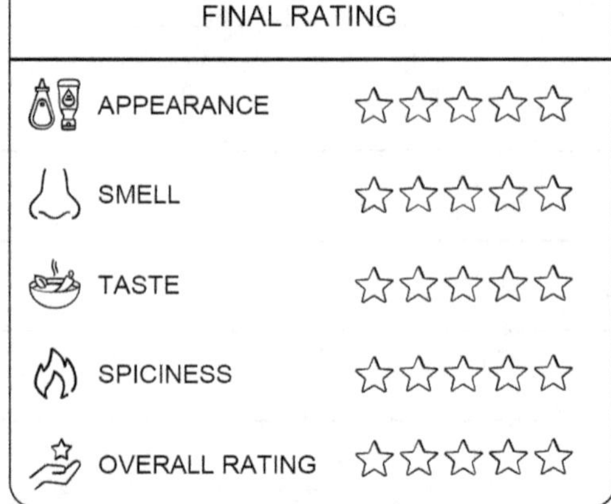

NAME	BRAND
ORIGIN	SAMPLED
SCOVILLE	TEXTURE
COLOR	PRICE

FLAVOR WHEEL

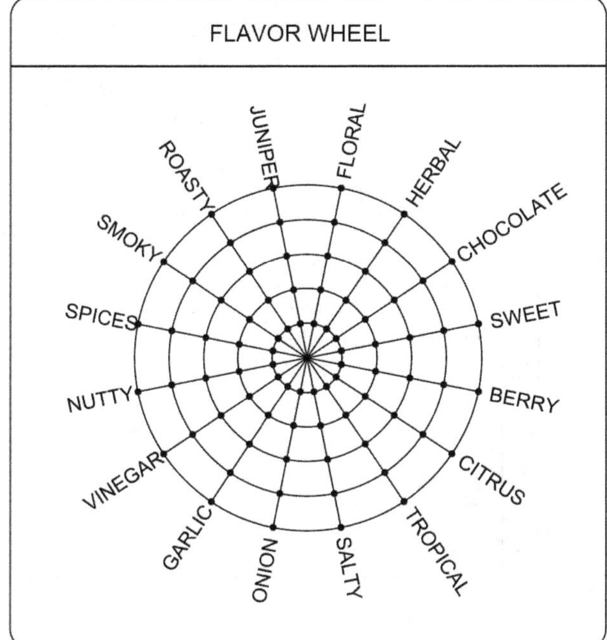

MAIN INGREDIENTS

HEAT METER

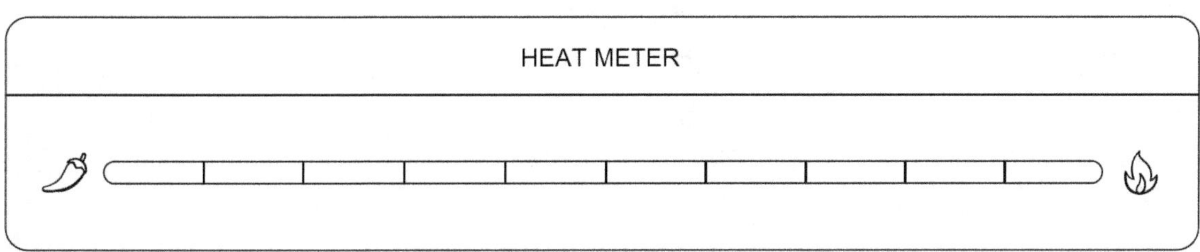

ADDITIONAL NOTES

FINAL RATING

APPEARANCE ☆☆☆☆☆

SMELL ☆☆☆☆☆

TASTE ☆☆☆☆☆

SPICINESS ☆☆☆☆☆

OVERALL RATING ☆☆☆☆☆

NAME	BRAND
ORIGIN	SAMPLED
SCOVILLE	TEXTURE
COLOR	PRICE

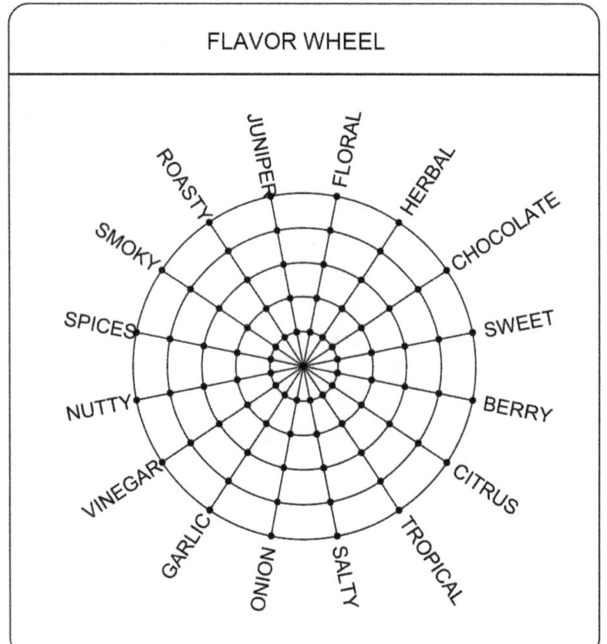

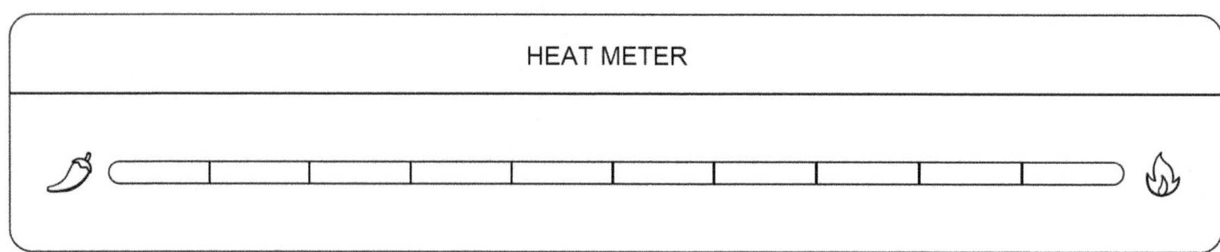

ADDITIONAL NOTES

NAME	BRAND
ORIGIN	SAMPLED
SCOVILLE	TEXTURE
COLOR	PRICE

FLAVOR WHEEL

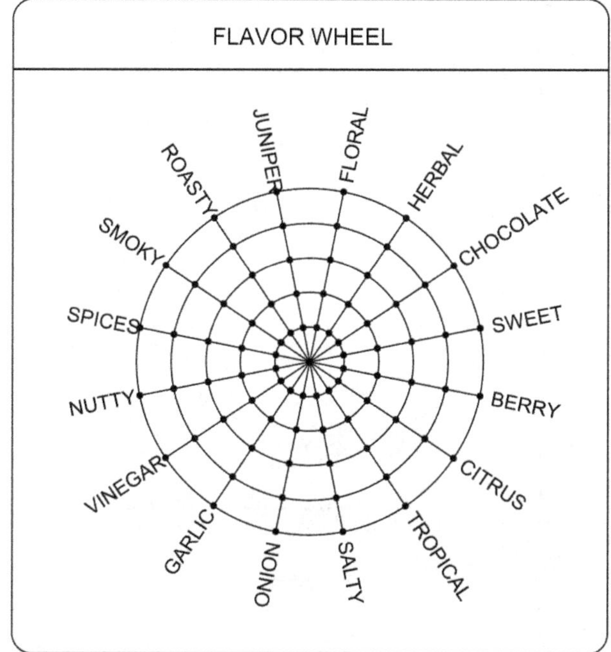

MAIN INGREDIENTS

HEAT METER

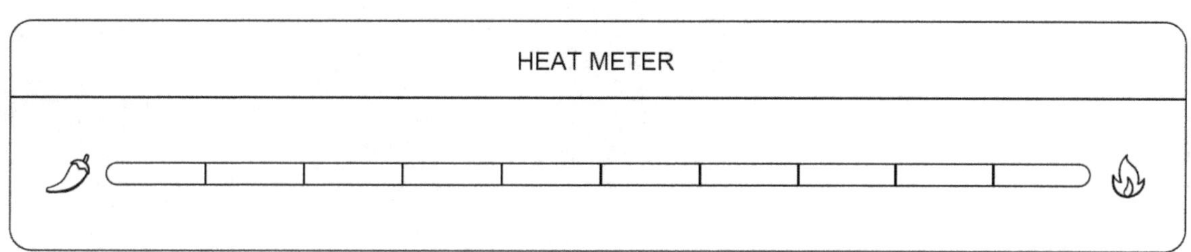

ADDITIONAL NOTES

FINAL RATING

APPEARANCE ☆☆☆☆☆

SMELL ☆☆☆☆☆

TASTE ☆☆☆☆☆

SPICINESS ☆☆☆☆☆

OVERALL RATING ☆☆☆☆☆

NAME	BRAND
ORIGIN	SAMPLED
SCOVILLE	TEXTURE
COLOR	PRICE

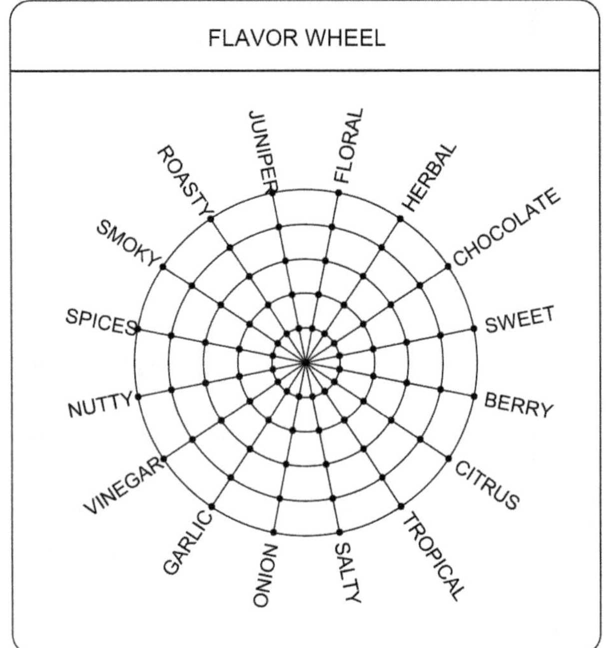

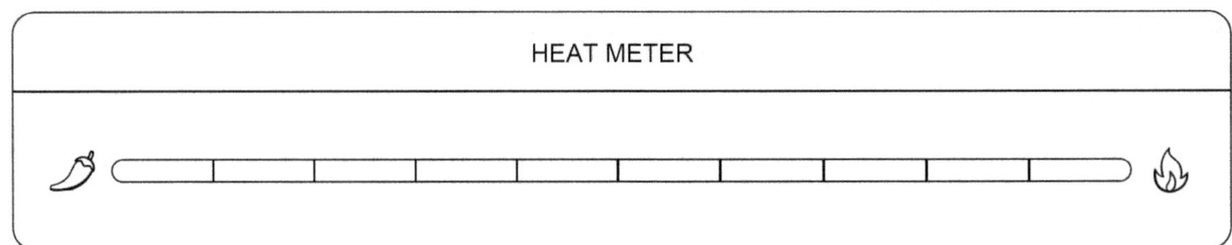

ADDITIONAL NOTES

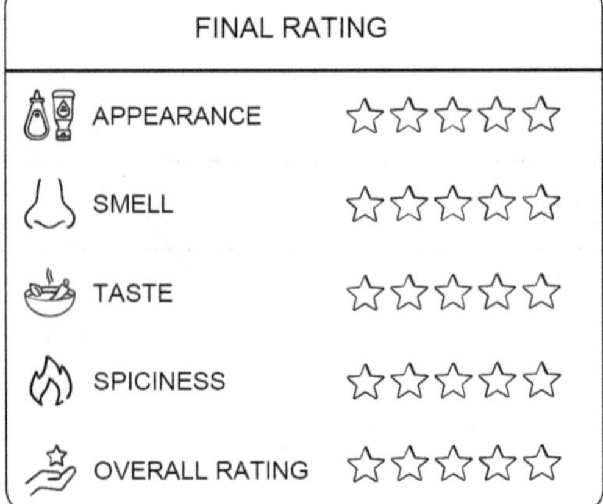

NAME	BRAND
ORIGIN	SAMPLED
SCOVILLE	TEXTURE
COLOR	PRICE

FLAVOR WHEEL

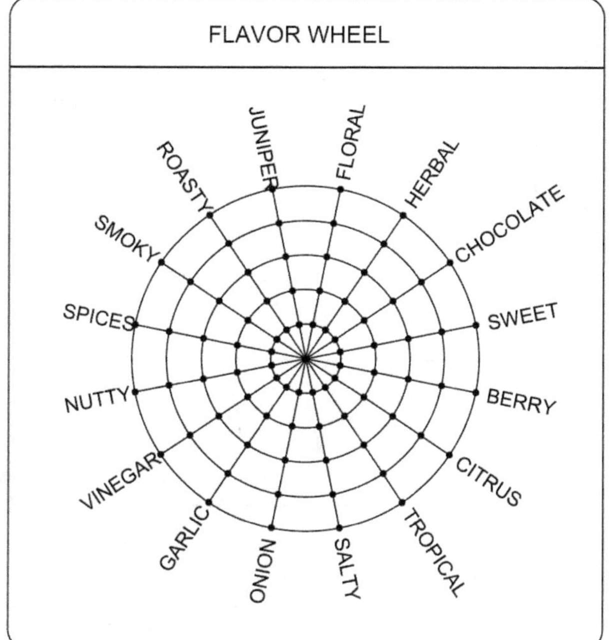

MAIN INGREDIENTS

HEAT METER

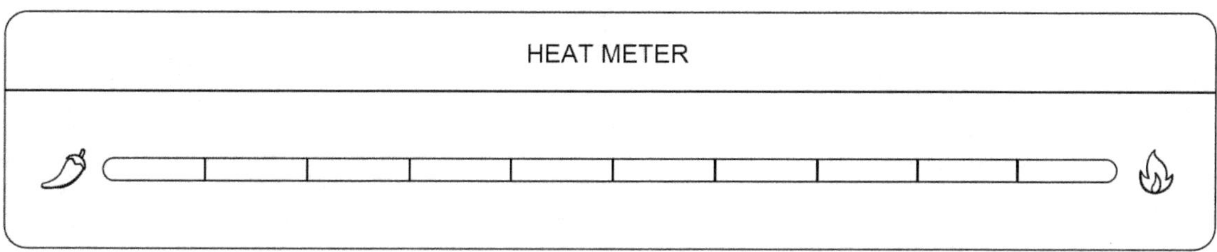

ADDITIONAL NOTES

FINAL RATING

APPEARANCE ☆☆☆☆☆

SMELL ☆☆☆☆☆

TASTE ☆☆☆☆☆

SPICINESS ☆☆☆☆☆

OVERALL RATING ☆☆☆☆☆

NAME	BRAND
ORIGIN	SAMPLED
SCOVILLE	TEXTURE
COLOR	PRICE

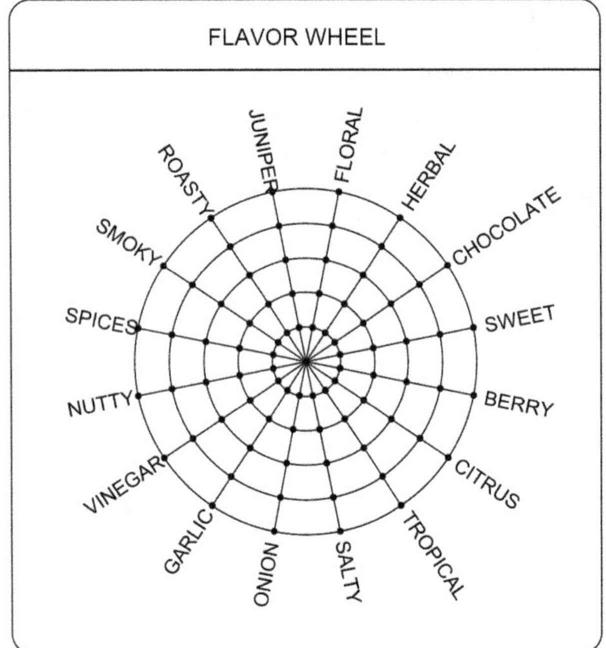

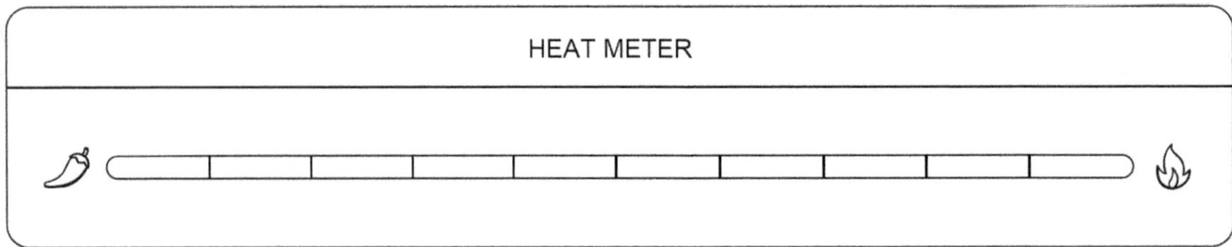

ADDITIONAL NOTES

FINAL RATING

APPEARANCE	☆☆☆☆☆
SMELL	☆☆☆☆☆
TASTE	☆☆☆☆☆
SPICINESS	☆☆☆☆☆
OVERALL RATING	☆☆☆☆☆

NAME	BRAND
ORIGIN	SAMPLED
SCOVILLE	TEXTURE
COLOR	PRICE

FLAVOR WHEEL

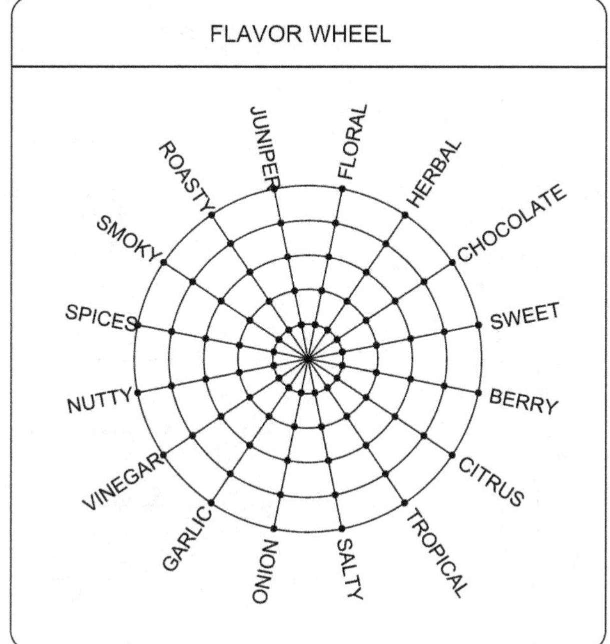

MAIN INGREDIENTS

HEAT METER

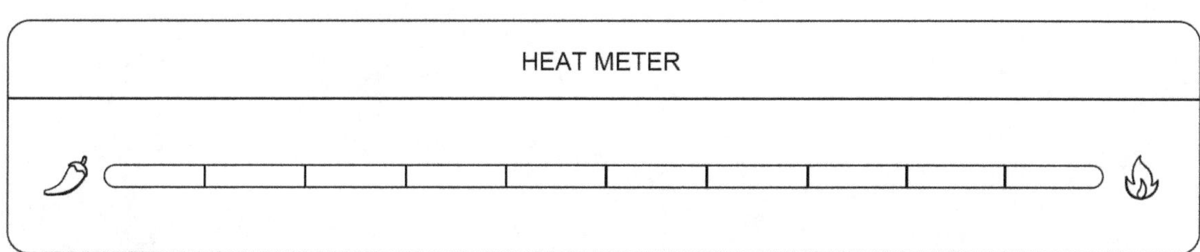

ADDITIONAL NOTES

FINAL RATING

APPEARANCE ☆☆☆☆☆

SMELL ☆☆☆☆☆

TASTE ☆☆☆☆☆

SPICINESS ☆☆☆☆☆

OVERALL RATING ☆☆☆☆☆

NAME	BRAND
ORIGIN	SAMPLED
SCOVILLE	TEXTURE
COLOR	PRICE

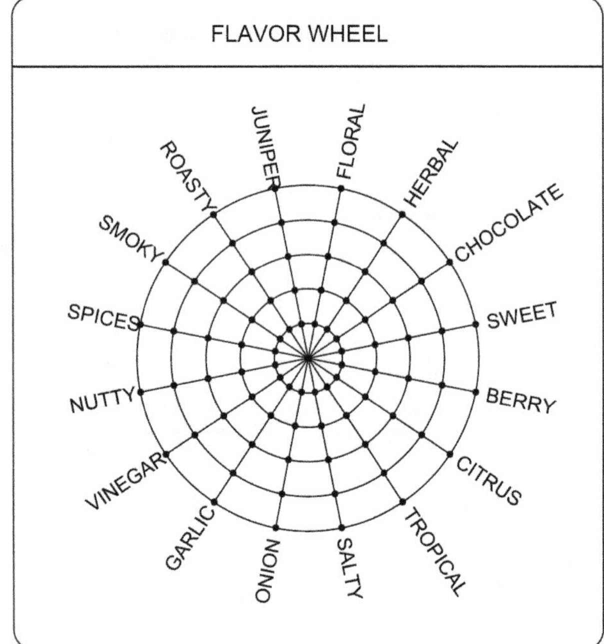

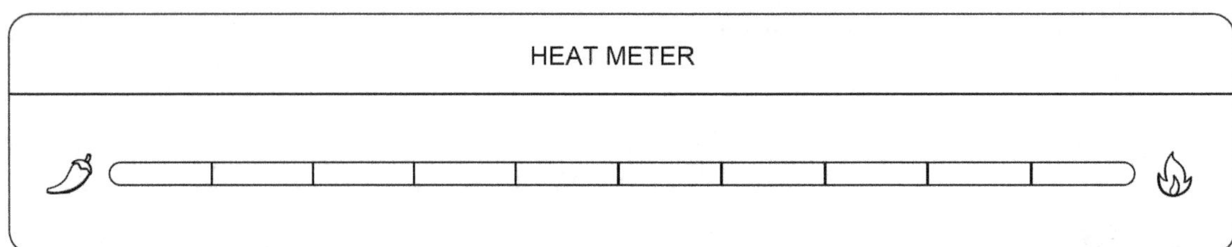

ADDITIONAL NOTES

NAME	BRAND
ORIGIN	SAMPLED
SCOVILLE	TEXTURE
COLOR	PRICE

FLAVOR WHEEL

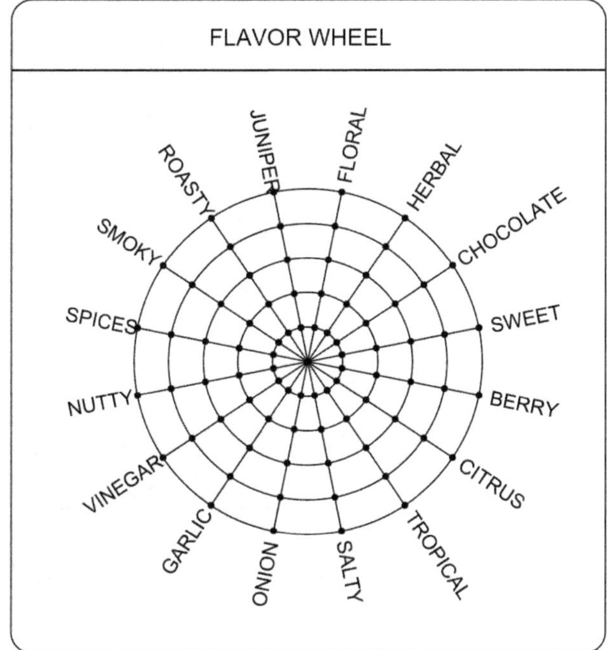

MAIN INGREDIENTS

HEAT METER

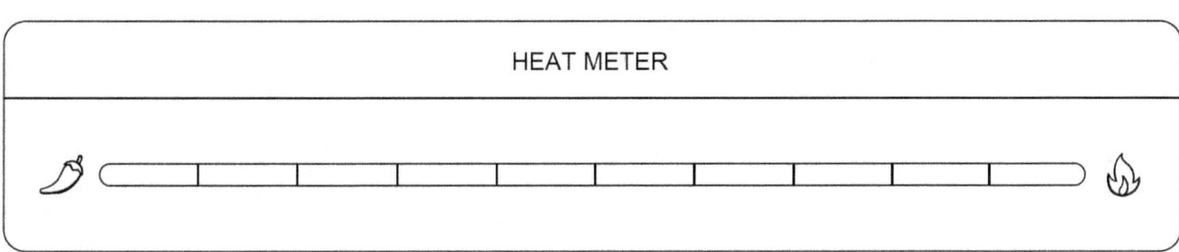

ADDITIONAL NOTES

FINAL RATING

NAME	BRAND
ORIGIN	SAMPLED
SCOVILLE	TEXTURE
COLOR	PRICE

FLAVOR WHEEL

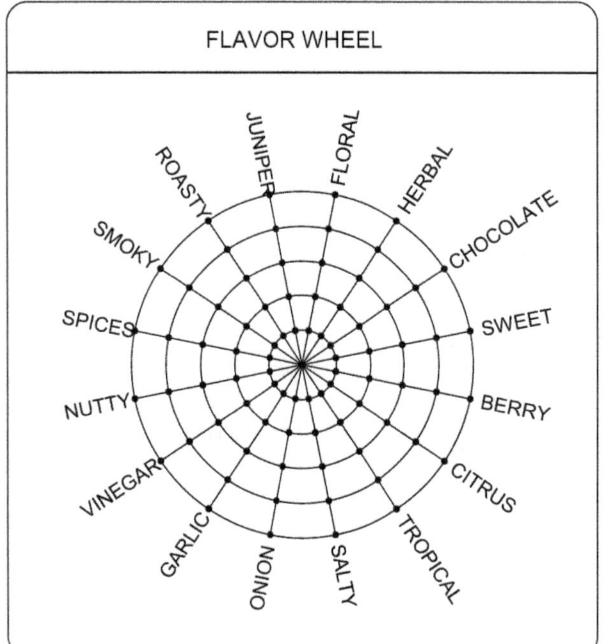

MAIN INGREDIENTS

HEAT METER

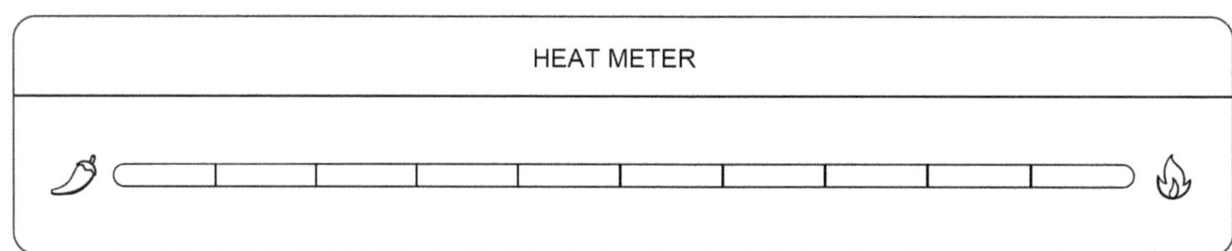

ADDITIONAL NOTES

FINAL RATING

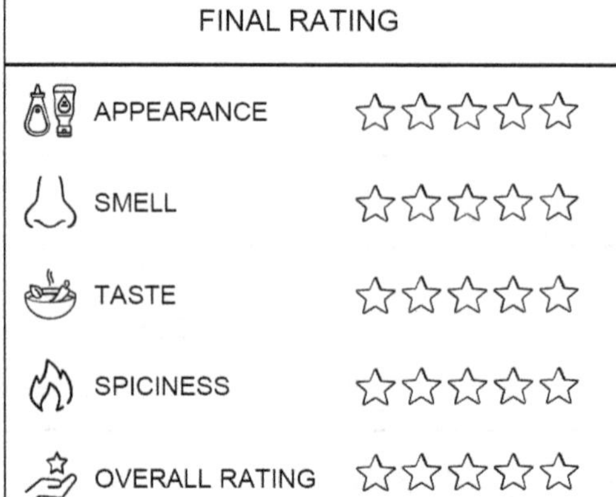

NAME	BRAND
ORIGIN	SAMPLED
SCOVILLE	TEXTURE
COLOR	PRICE

FLAVOR WHEEL

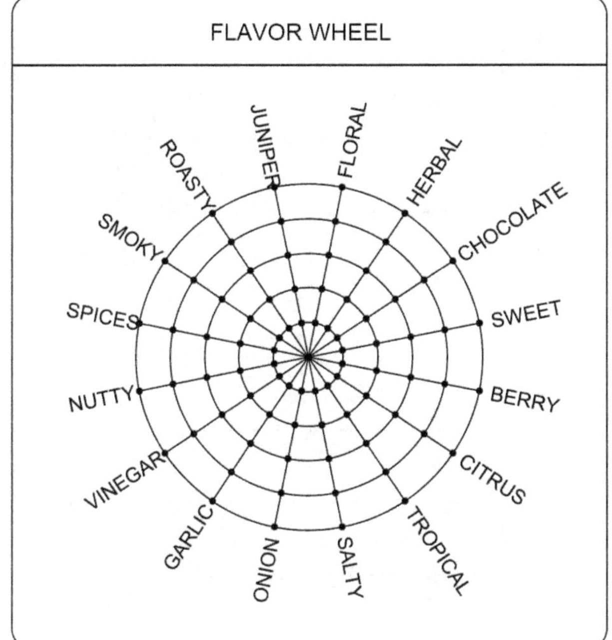

MAIN INGREDIENTS

HEAT METER

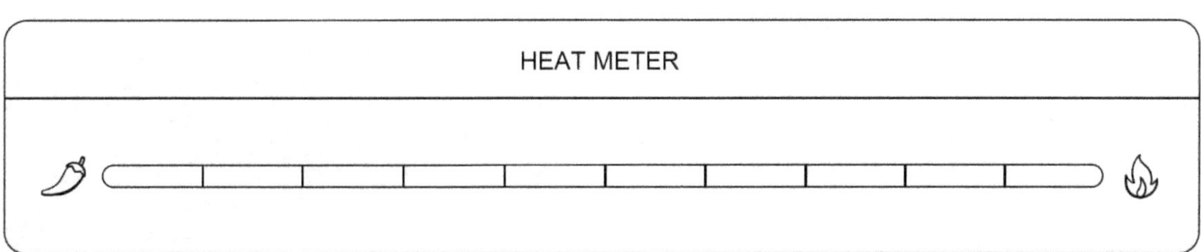

ADDITIONAL NOTES

FINAL RATING

APPEARANCE ☆☆☆☆☆

SMELL ☆☆☆☆☆

TASTE ☆☆☆☆☆

SPICINESS ☆☆☆☆☆

OVERALL RATING ☆☆☆☆☆

NAME	BRAND
ORIGIN	SAMPLED
SCOVILLE	TEXTURE
COLOR	PRICE

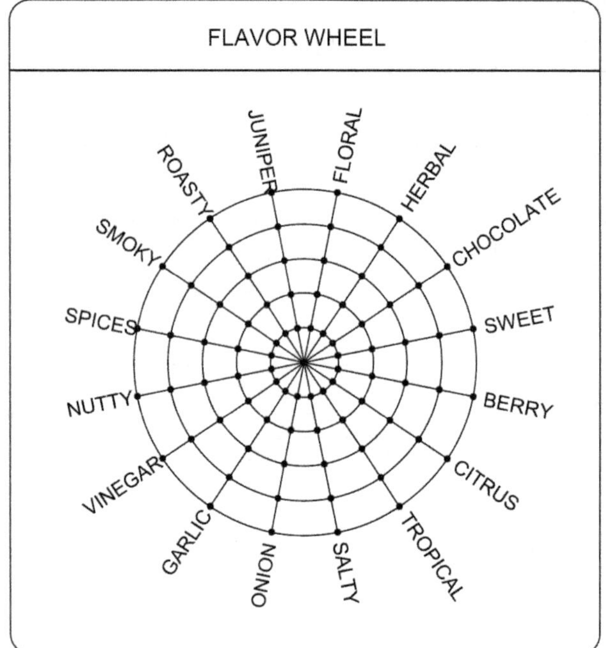

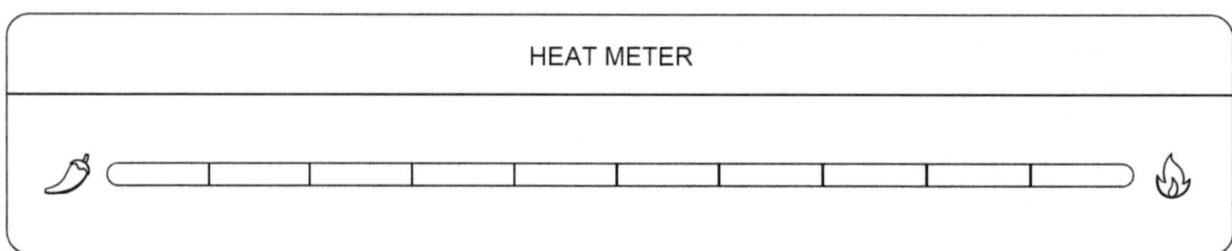

ADDITIONAL NOTES

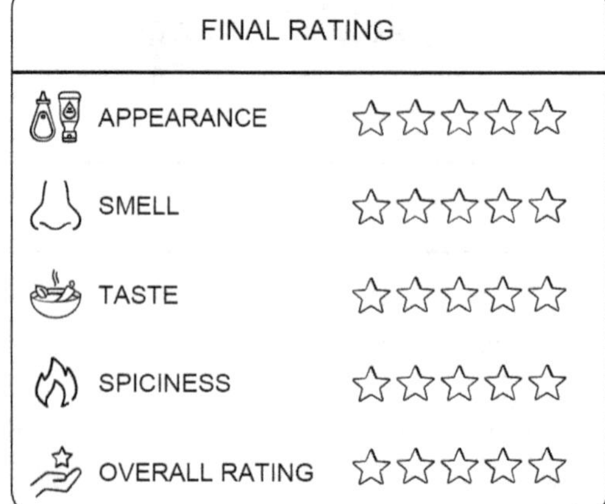

NAME	BRAND
ORIGIN	SAMPLED
SCOVILLE	TEXTURE
COLOR	PRICE

FLAVOR WHEEL

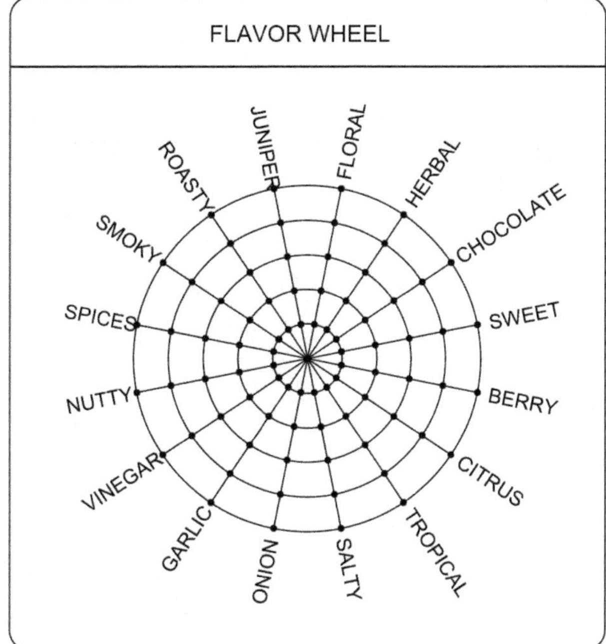

MAIN INGREDIENTS

HEAT METER

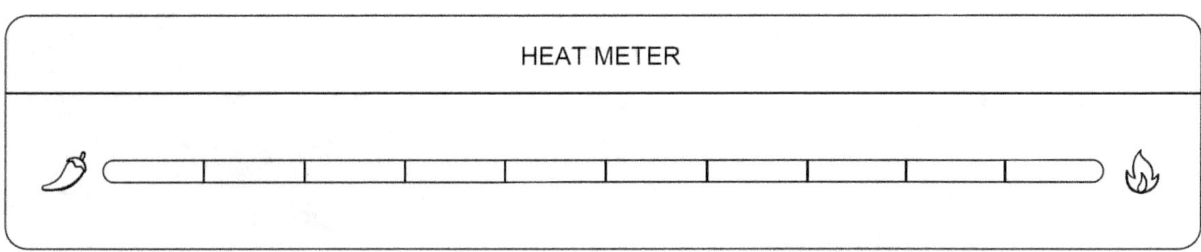

ADDITIONAL NOTES

FINAL RATING

- APPEARANCE ☆☆☆☆☆
- SMELL ☆☆☆☆☆
- TASTE ☆☆☆☆☆
- SPICINESS ☆☆☆☆☆
- OVERALL RATING ☆☆☆☆☆

NAME	BRAND
ORIGIN	SAMPLED
SCOVILLE	TEXTURE
COLOR	PRICE

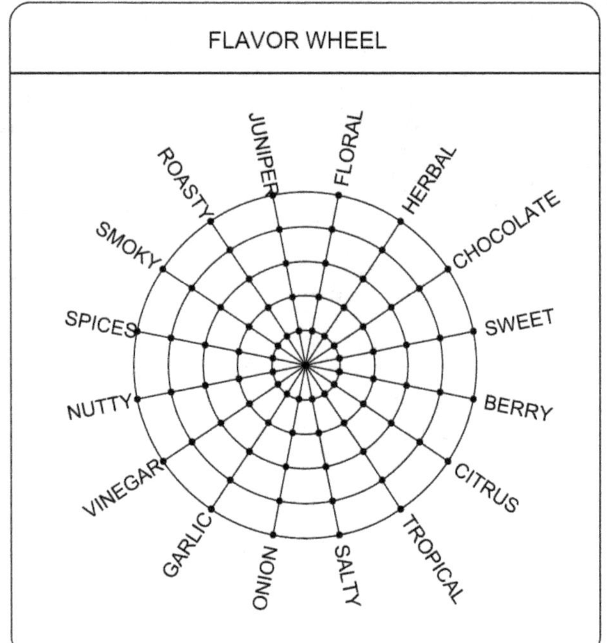

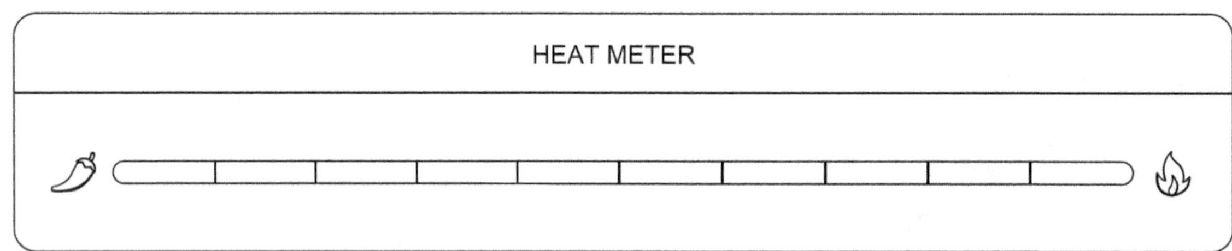

ADDITIONAL NOTES

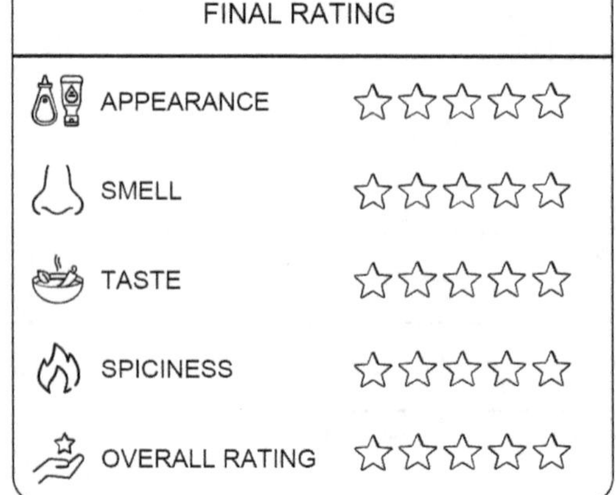

NAME	BRAND
ORIGIN	SAMPLED
SCOVILLE	TEXTURE
COLOR	PRICE

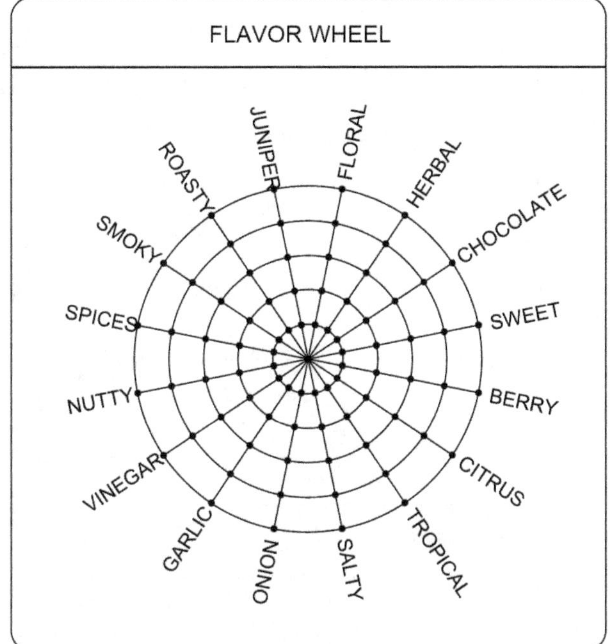

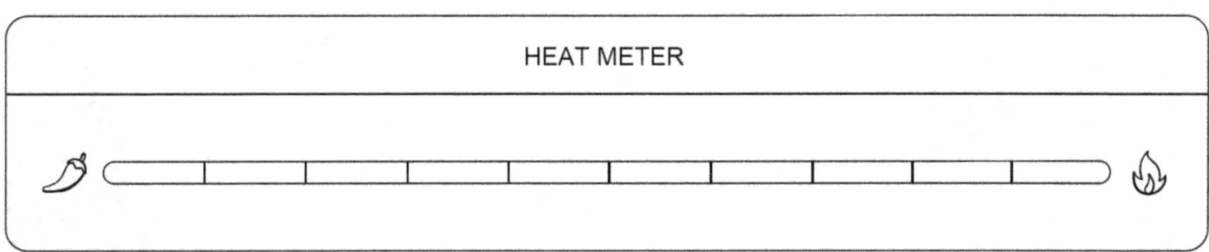

ADDITIONAL NOTES

FINAL RATING

APPEARANCE	☆☆☆☆☆
SMELL	☆☆☆☆☆
TASTE	☆☆☆☆☆
SPICINESS	☆☆☆☆☆
OVERALL RATING	☆☆☆☆☆

NAME	BRAND
ORIGIN	SAMPLED
SCOVILLE	TEXTURE
COLOR	PRICE

FLAVOR WHEEL

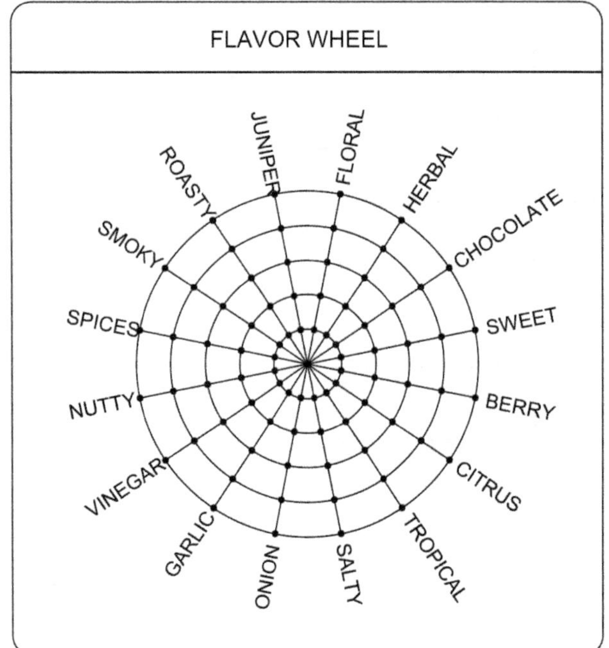

MAIN INGREDIENTS

HEAT METER

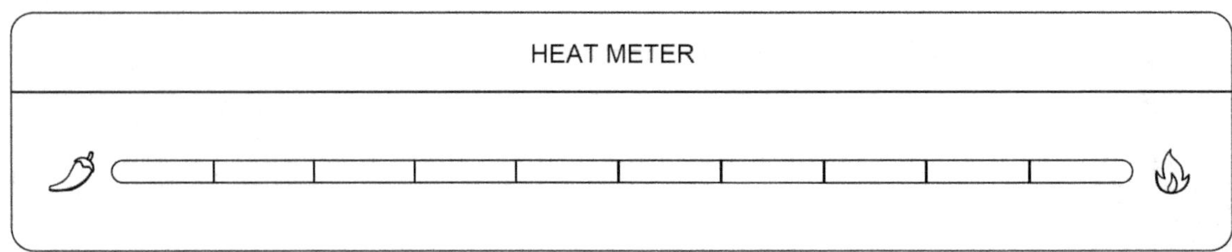

ADDITIONAL NOTES

FINAL RATING

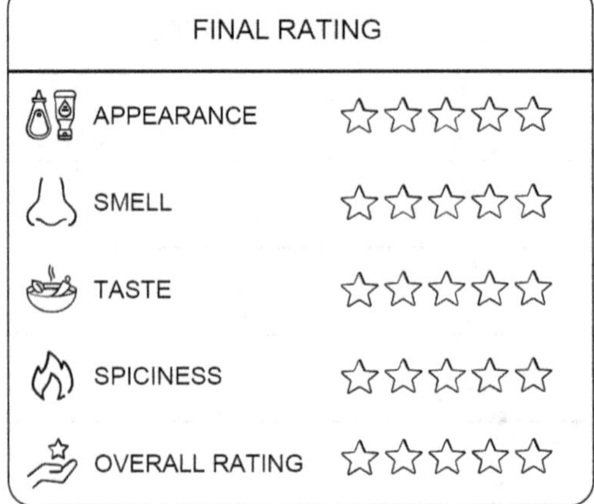

NAME	BRAND
ORIGIN	SAMPLED
SCOVILLE	TEXTURE
COLOR	PRICE

FLAVOR WHEEL

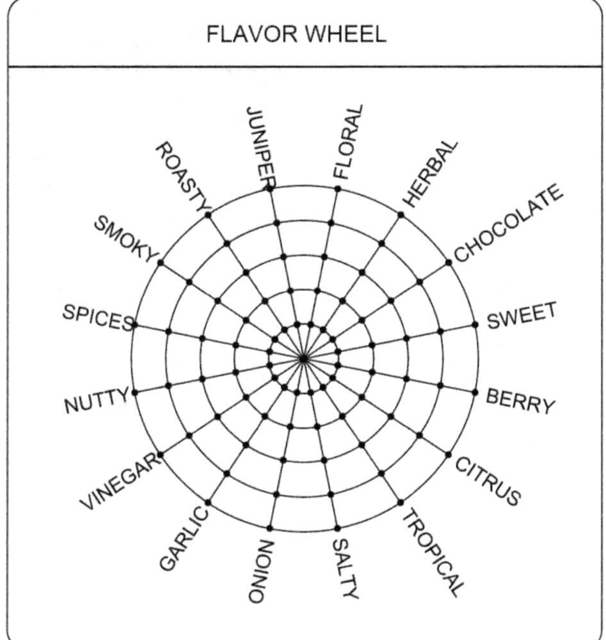

MAIN INGREDIENTS

HEAT METER

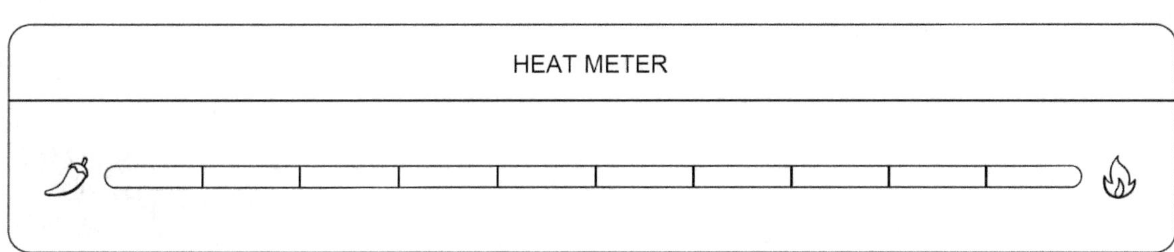

ADDITIONAL NOTES

FINAL RATING

APPEARANCE ☆☆☆☆☆

SMELL ☆☆☆☆☆

TASTE ☆☆☆☆☆

SPICINESS ☆☆☆☆☆

OVERALL RATING ☆☆☆☆☆

NAME	BRAND
ORIGIN	SAMPLED
SCOVILLE	TEXTURE
COLOR	PRICE

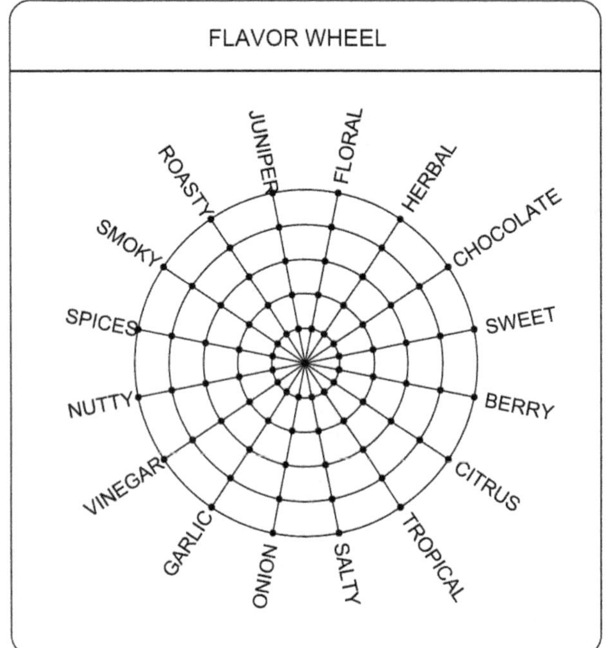

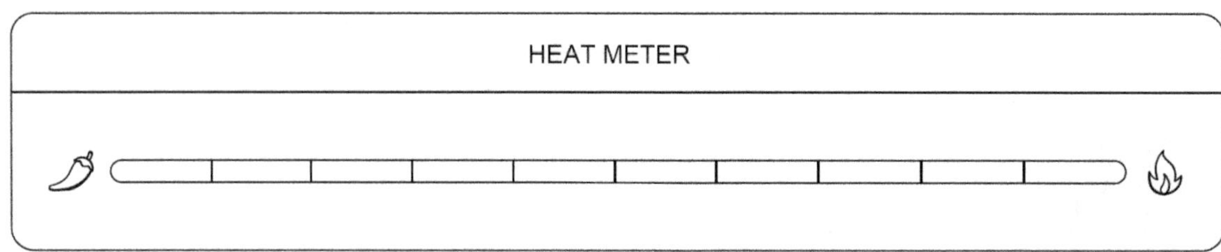

ADDITIONAL NOTES

NAME	BRAND
ORIGIN	SAMPLED
SCOVILLE	TEXTURE
COLOR	PRICE

FLAVOR WHEEL

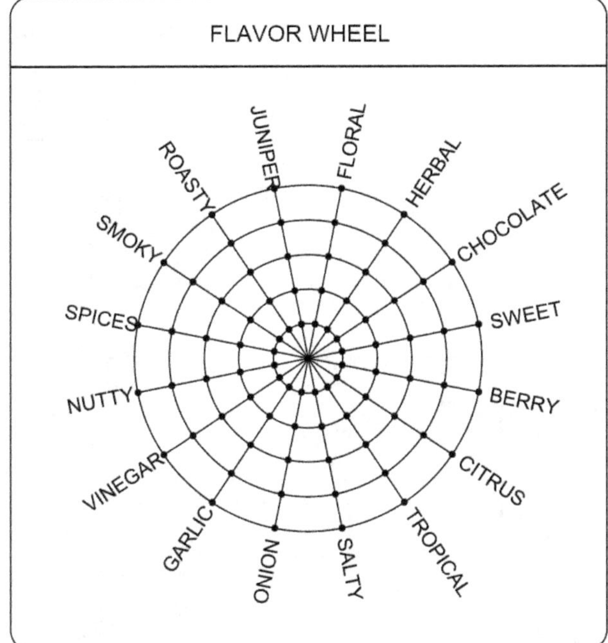

MAIN INGREDIENTS

HEAT METER

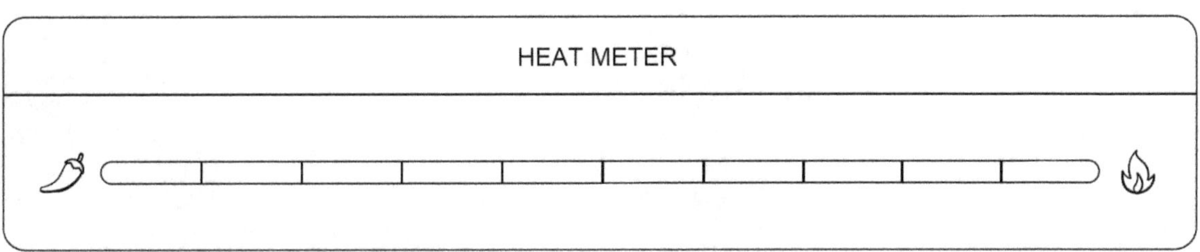

ADDITIONAL NOTES

FINAL RATING

APPEARANCE ☆☆☆☆☆

SMELL ☆☆☆☆☆

TASTE ☆☆☆☆☆

SPICINESS ☆☆☆☆☆

OVERALL RATING ☆☆☆☆☆

NAME	BRAND
ORIGIN	SAMPLED
SCOVILLE	TEXTURE
COLOR	PRICE

FLAVOR WHEEL

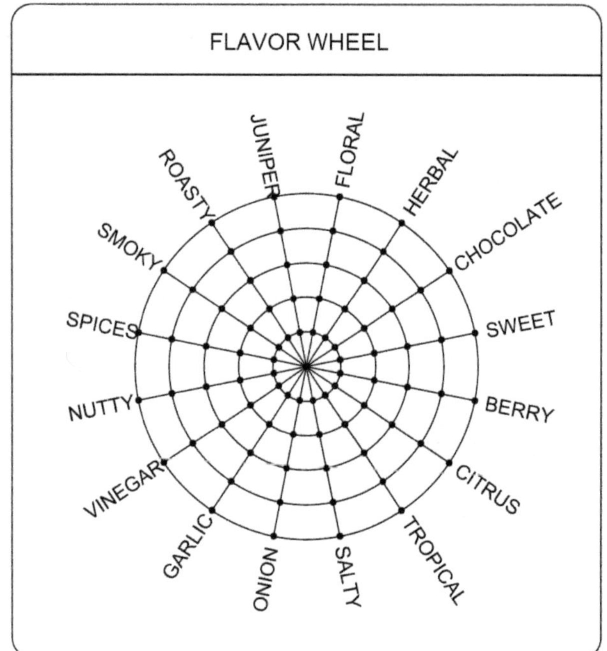

MAIN INGREDIENTS

HEAT METER

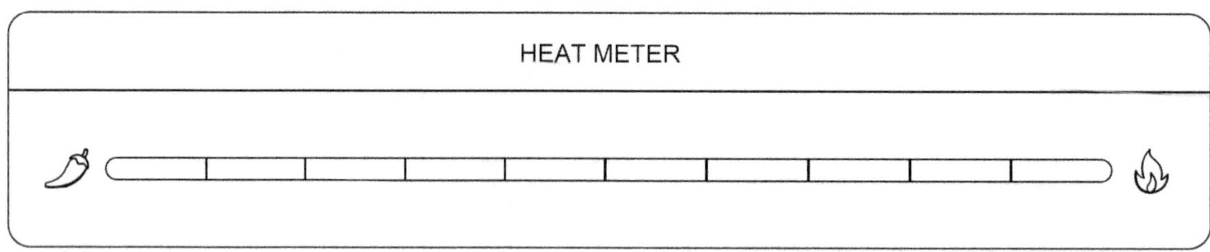

ADDITIONAL NOTES

FINAL RATING

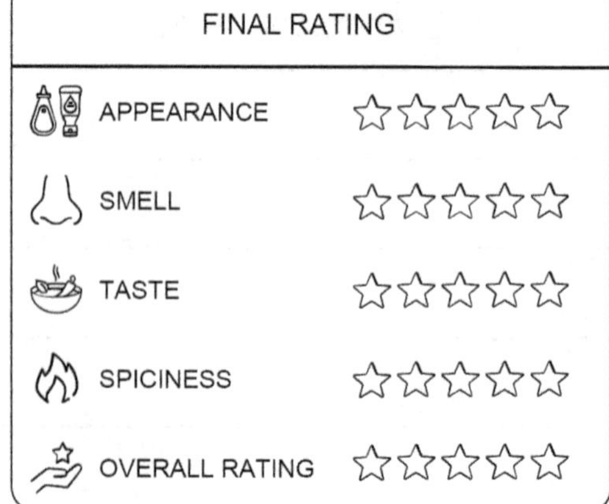

NAME	BRAND
ORIGIN	SAMPLED
SCOVILLE	TEXTURE
COLOR	PRICE

FLAVOR WHEEL

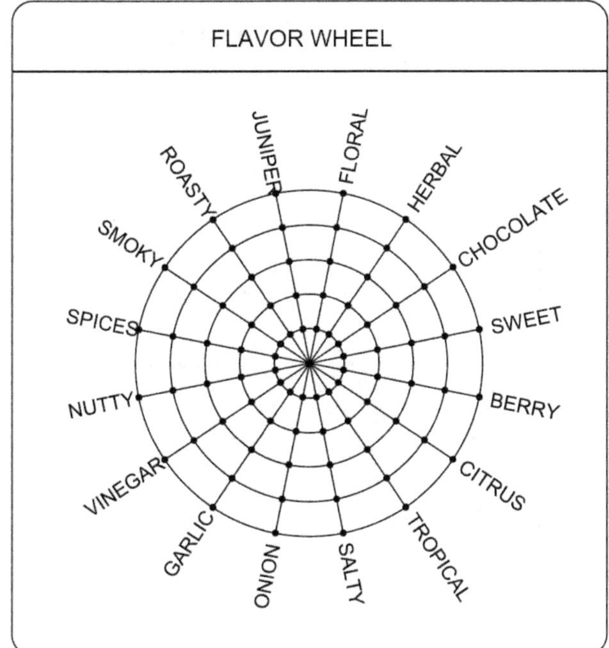

MAIN INGREDIENTS

HEAT METER

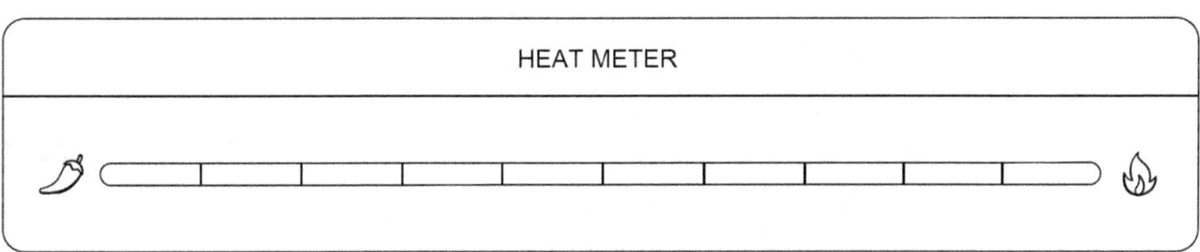

ADDITIONAL NOTES

FINAL RATING

APPEARANCE	☆☆☆☆☆
SMELL	☆☆☆☆☆
TASTE	☆☆☆☆☆
SPICINESS	☆☆☆☆☆
OVERALL RATING	☆☆☆☆☆

NAME	BRAND
ORIGIN	SAMPLED
SCOVILLE	TEXTURE
COLOR	PRICE

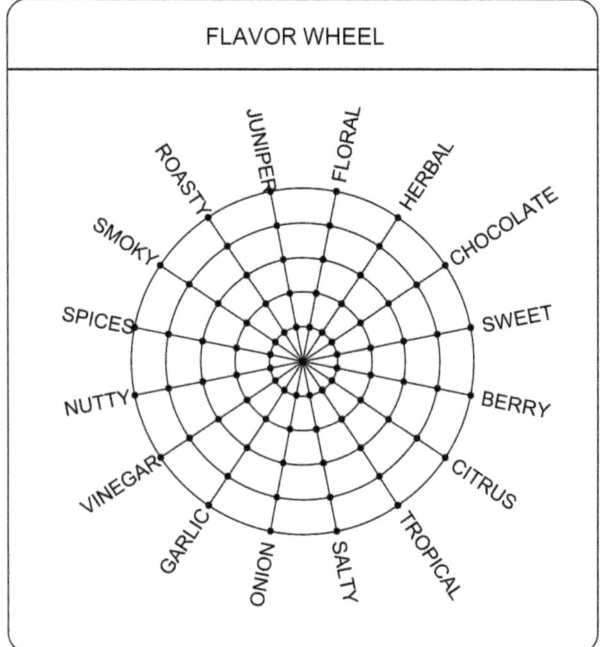

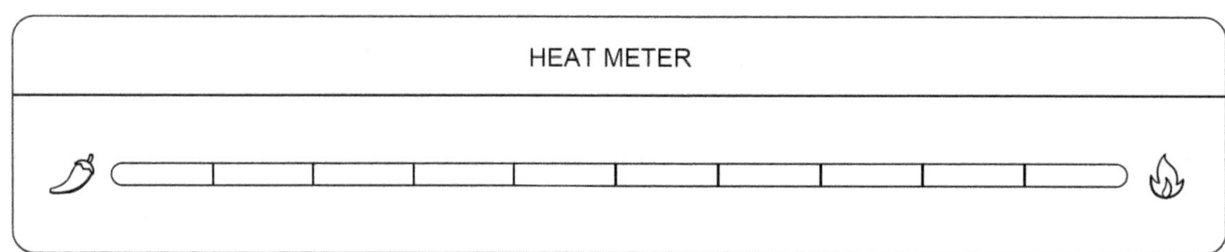

ADDITIONAL NOTES

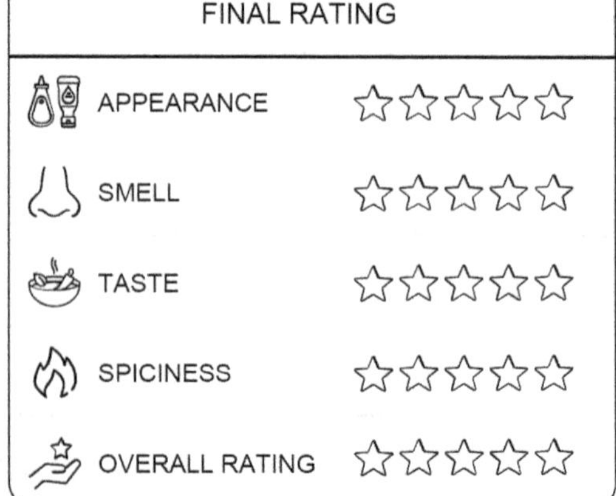

NAME	BRAND
ORIGIN	SAMPLED
SCOVILLE	TEXTURE
COLOR	PRICE

FLAVOR WHEEL

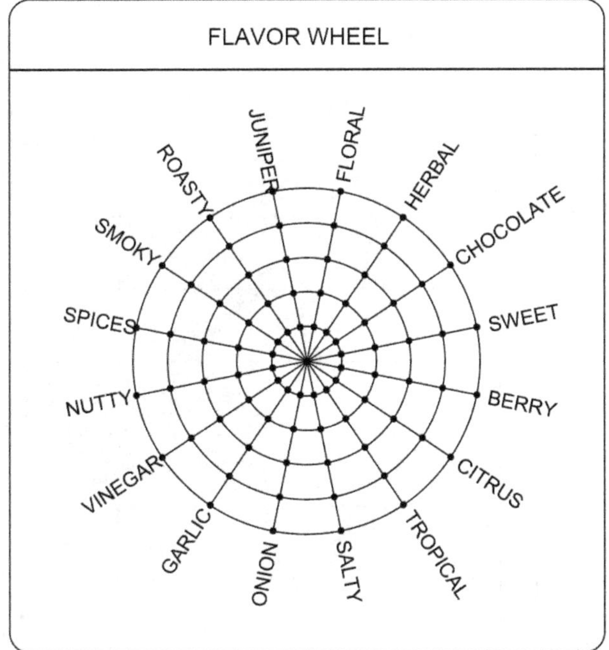

MAIN INGREDIENTS

HEAT METER

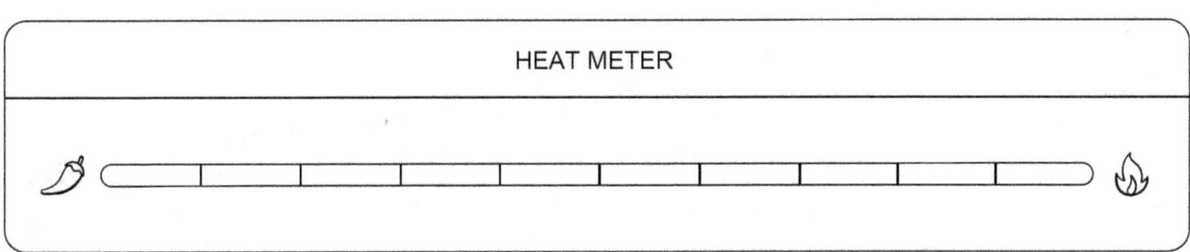

ADDITIONAL NOTES

FINAL RATING

APPEARANCE ☆☆☆☆☆

SMELL ☆☆☆☆☆

TASTE ☆☆☆☆☆

SPICINESS ☆☆☆☆☆

OVERALL RATING ☆☆☆☆☆

NAME	BRAND
ORIGIN	SAMPLED
SCOVILLE	TEXTURE
COLOR	PRICE

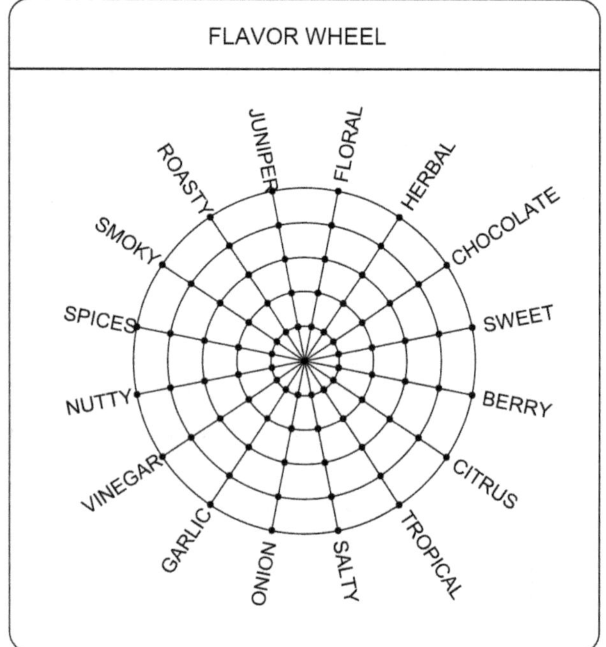

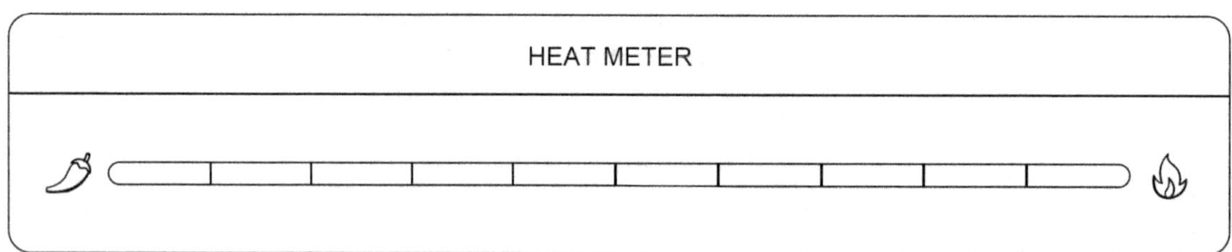

ADDITIONAL NOTES

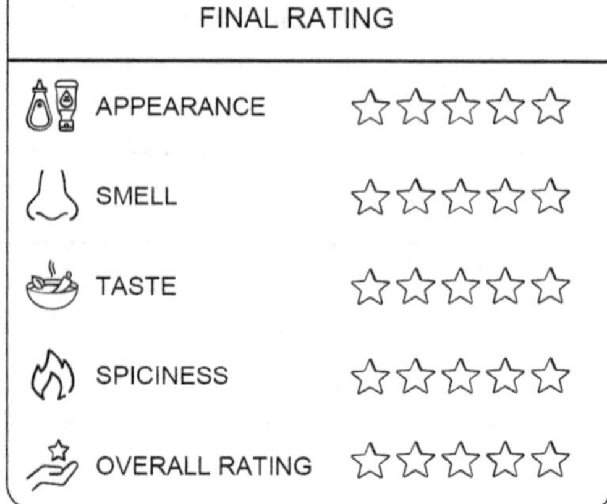

NAME	BRAND
ORIGIN	SAMPLED
SCOVILLE	TEXTURE
COLOR	PRICE

FLAVOR WHEEL

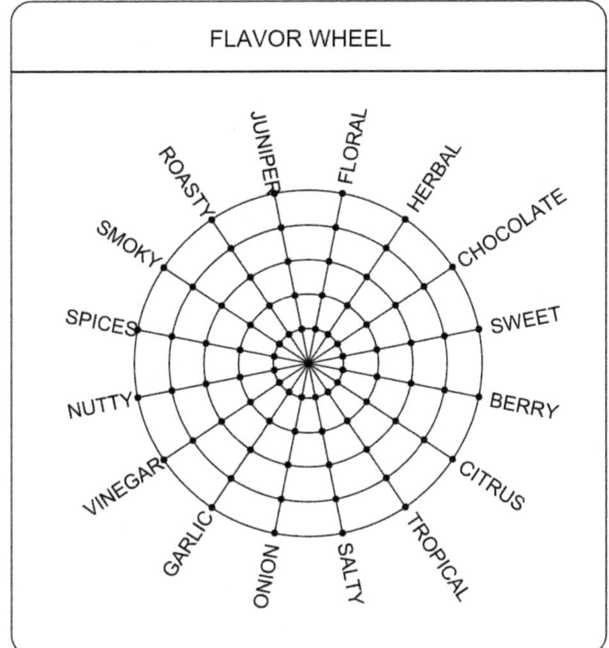

MAIN INGREDIENTS

HEAT METER

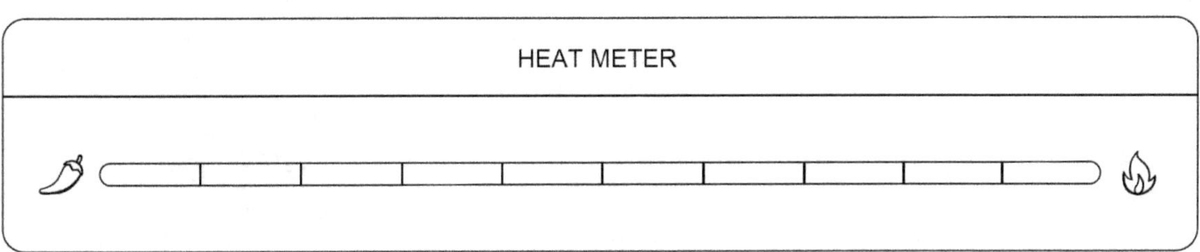

ADDITIONAL NOTES

FINAL RATING

APPEARANCE ☆☆☆☆☆

SMELL ☆☆☆☆☆

TASTE ☆☆☆☆☆

SPICINESS ☆☆☆☆☆

OVERALL RATING ☆☆☆☆☆

NAME	BRAND
ORIGIN	SAMPLED
SCOVILLE	TEXTURE
COLOR	PRICE

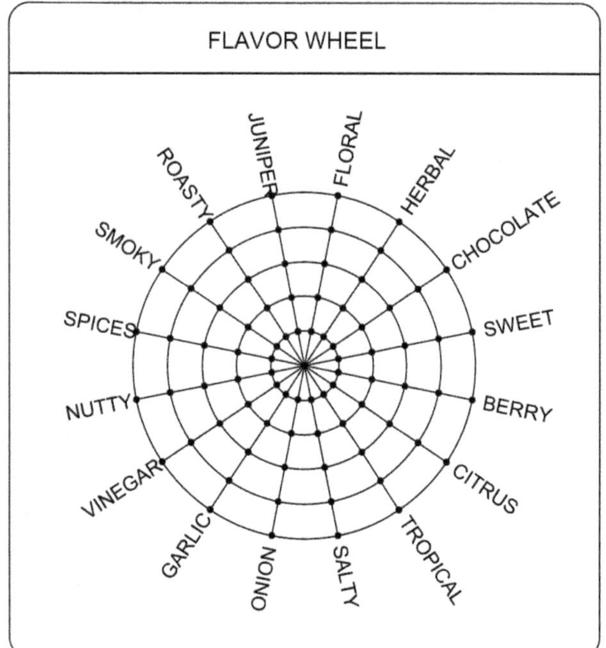

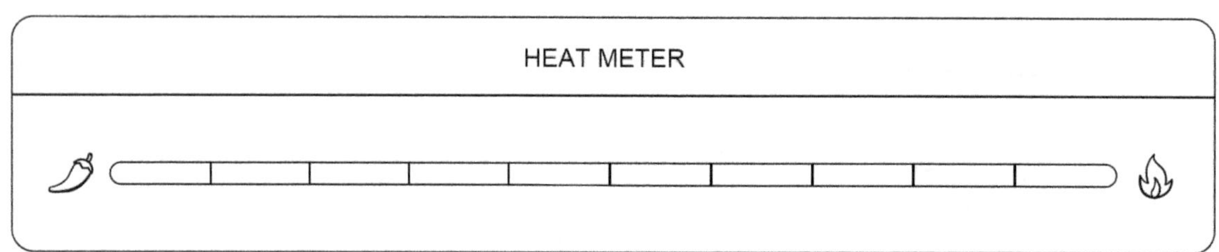

ADDITIONAL NOTES

NAME	BRAND
ORIGIN	SAMPLED
SCOVILLE	TEXTURE
COLOR	PRICE

FLAVOR WHEEL

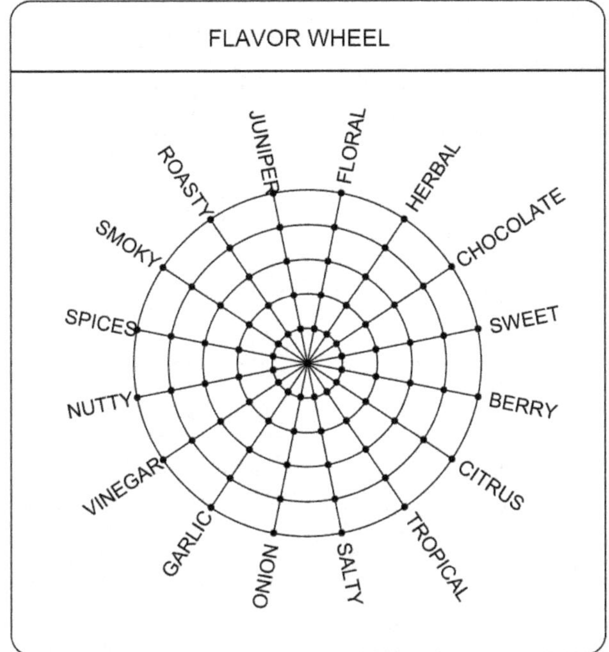

MAIN INGREDIENTS

HEAT METER

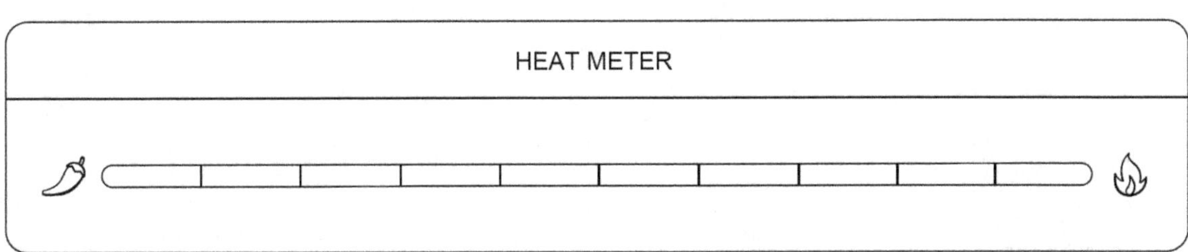

ADDITIONAL NOTES

FINAL RATING

APPEARANCE ☆☆☆☆☆

SMELL ☆☆☆☆☆

TASTE ☆☆☆☆☆

SPICINESS ☆☆☆☆☆

OVERALL RATING ☆☆☆☆☆

NAME	BRAND
ORIGIN	SAMPLED
SCOVILLE	TEXTURE
COLOR	PRICE

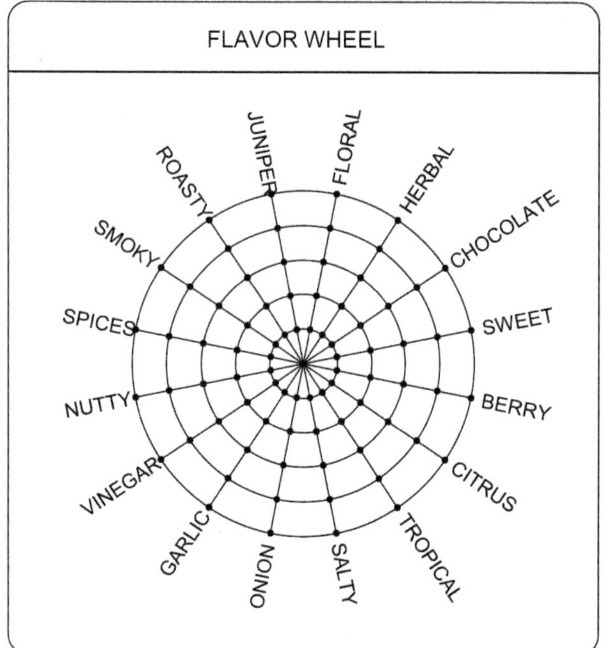

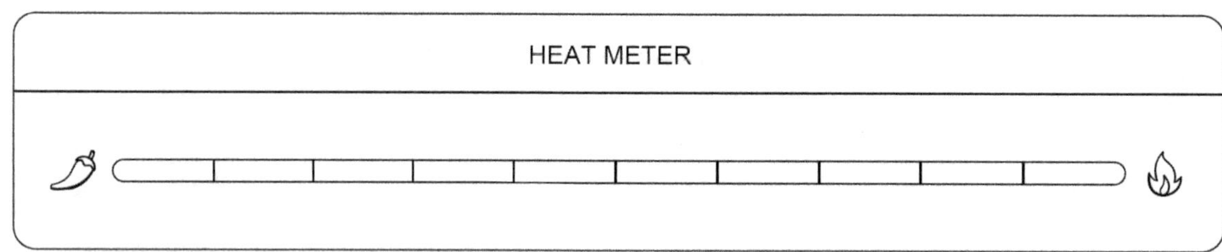

ADDITIONAL NOTES

NAME	BRAND
ORIGIN	SAMPLED
SCOVILLE	TEXTURE
COLOR	PRICE

FLAVOR WHEEL

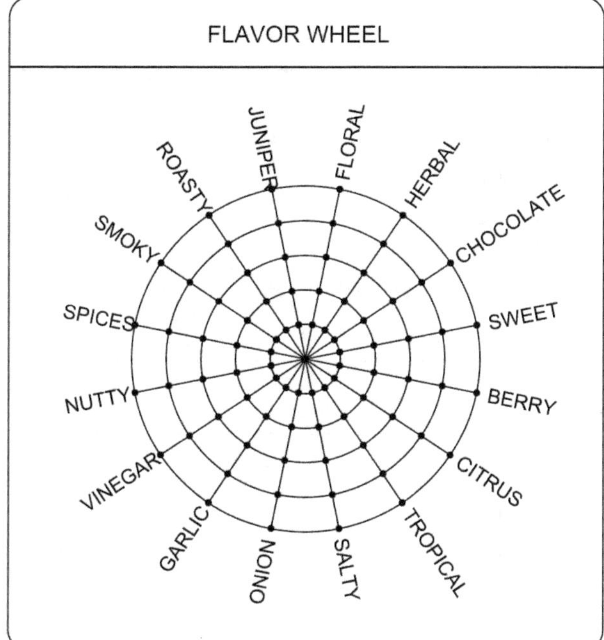

MAIN INGREDIENTS

HEAT METER

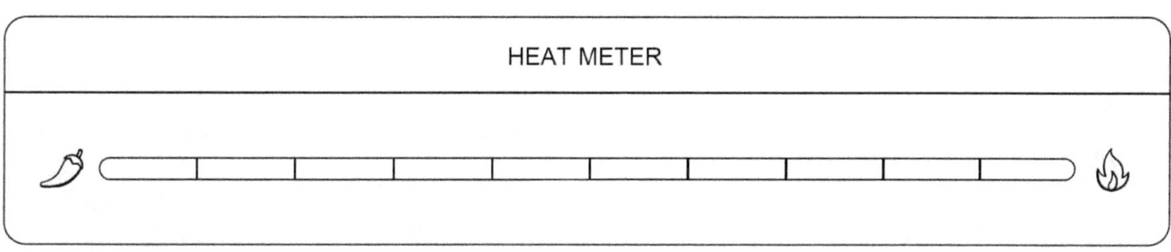

ADDITIONAL NOTES

FINAL RATING

APPEARANCE ☆☆☆☆☆

SMELL ☆☆☆☆☆

TASTE ☆☆☆☆☆

SPICINESS ☆☆☆☆☆

OVERALL RATING ☆☆☆☆☆

NAME	BRAND
ORIGIN	SAMPLED
SCOVILLE	TEXTURE
COLOR	PRICE

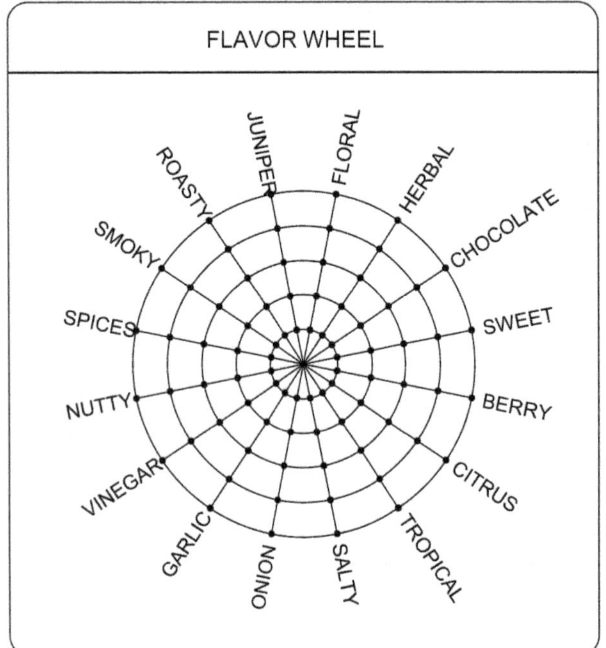

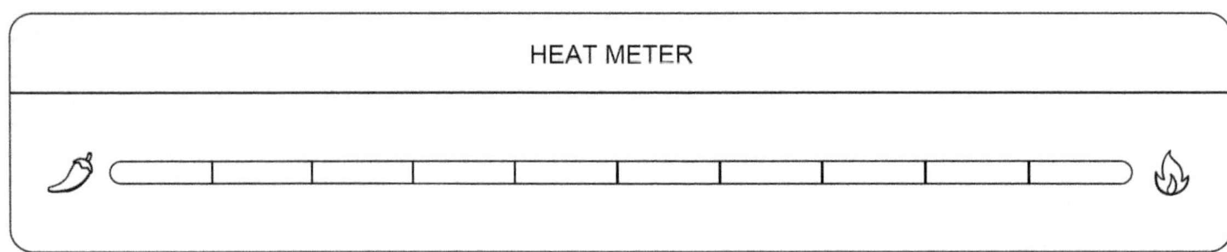

ADDITIONAL NOTES

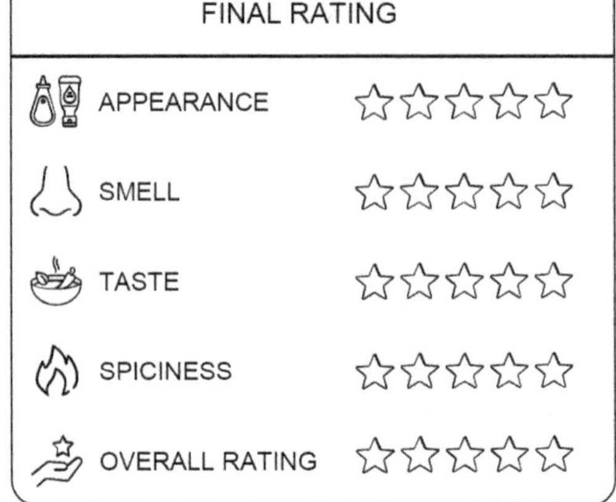

NAME	BRAND
ORIGIN	SAMPLED
SCOVILLE	TEXTURE
COLOR	PRICE

FLAVOR WHEEL

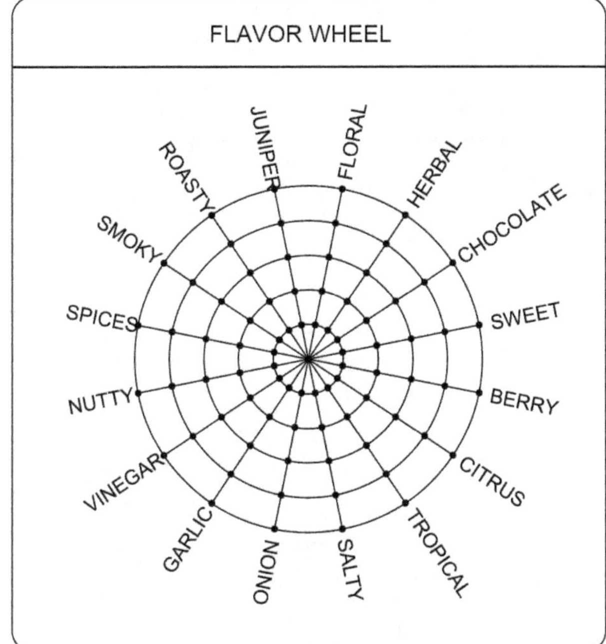

MAIN INGREDIENTS

HEAT METER

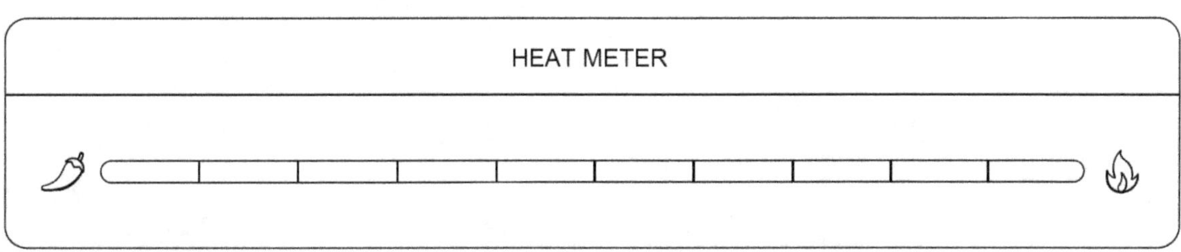

ADDITIONAL NOTES

FINAL RATING

APPEARANCE ☆☆☆☆☆

SMELL ☆☆☆☆☆

TASTE ☆☆☆☆☆

SPICINESS ☆☆☆☆☆

OVERALL RATING ☆☆☆☆☆

NAME	BRAND
ORIGIN	SAMPLED
SCOVILLE	TEXTURE
COLOR	PRICE

FLAVOR WHEEL

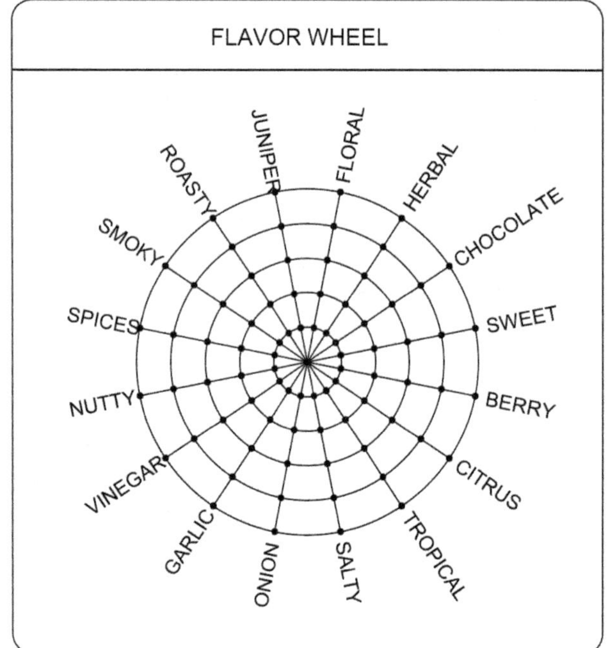

MAIN INGREDIENTS

HEAT METER

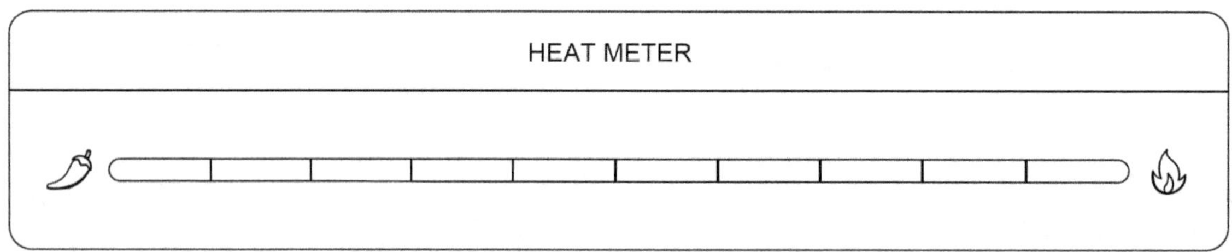

ADDITIONAL NOTES

FINAL RATING

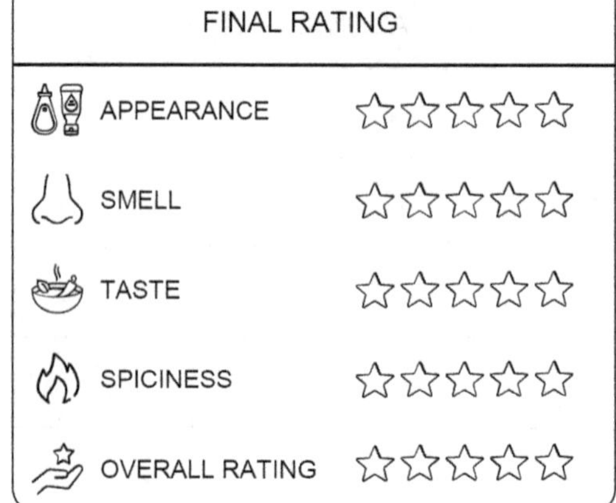

NAME	BRAND
ORIGIN	SAMPLED
SCOVILLE	TEXTURE
COLOR	PRICE

FLAVOR WHEEL

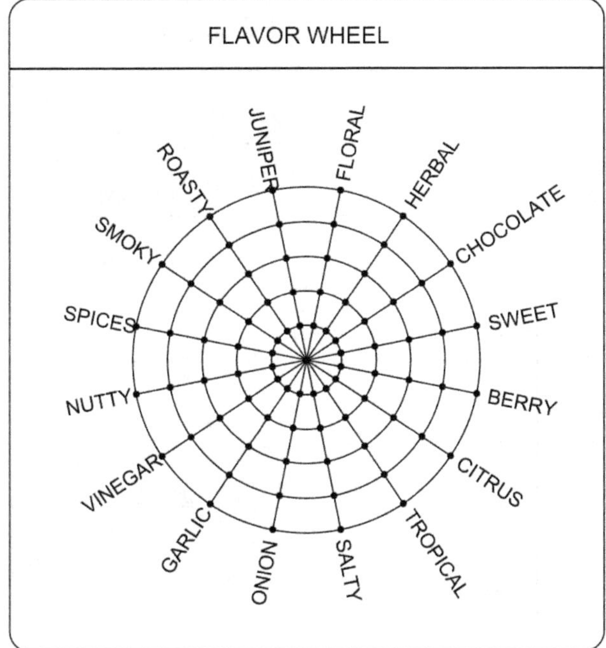

MAIN INGREDIENTS

HEAT METER

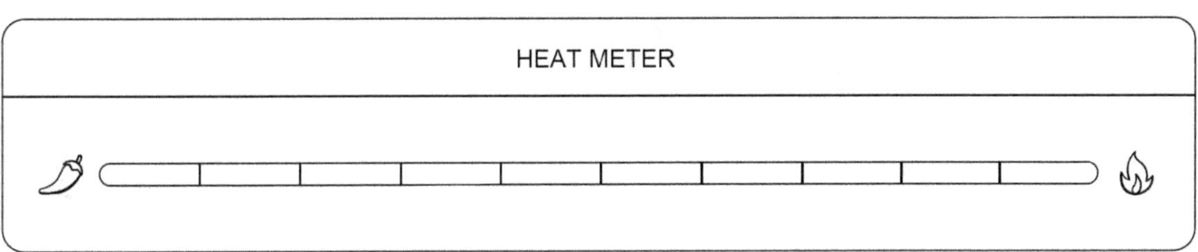

ADDITIONAL NOTES

FINAL RATING

APPEARANCE ☆☆☆☆☆

SMELL ☆☆☆☆☆

TASTE ☆☆☆☆☆

SPICINESS ☆☆☆☆☆

OVERALL RATING ☆☆☆☆☆

NAME	BRAND
ORIGIN	SAMPLED
SCOVILLE	TEXTURE
COLOR	PRICE

FLAVOR WHEEL

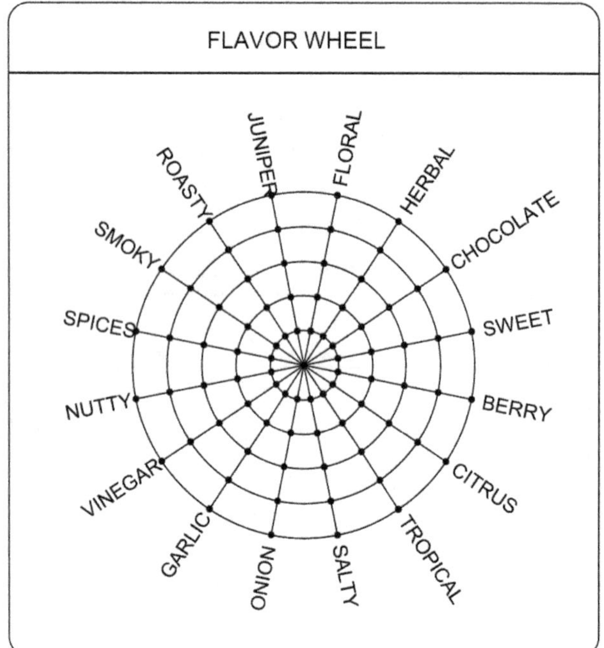

MAIN INGREDIENTS

HEAT METER

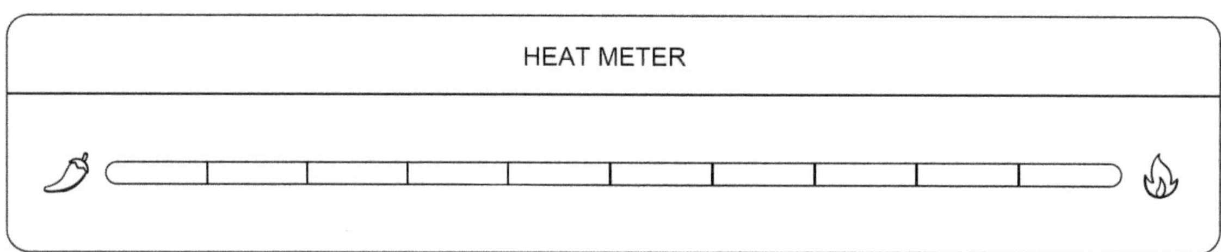

ADDITIONAL NOTES

FINAL RATING

CPSIA information can be obtained
at www.ICGtesting.com
Printed in the USA
LVHW051951090820
662602LV00005B/175